Emotional

MW01290895

By the same author

Dark Psychology and Manipulation

Emotional Intelligence Mastery

Empath (online from July 2020)

Emotional Intelligence

For a Better Life, success at work, and happier relationships. Improve Your Social Skills, Emotional Agility and Discover Why it Can Matter More Than IQ. (EQ 2.0)

PUBLISHED BY: Brandon Goleman

© **Copyright 2019 - All rights reserved.**

ISBN: 978-10-7797-213-1

First Edition: June 2019

Second Edition: May 2020

The content contained within this book may not be reproduced, duplicated, or transmitted without direct written permission from the author or the publisher.

Under no circumstances will any blame or legal responsibility be held against the publisher, or author, for any damages, reparation, or monetary loss due to the information contained within this book, either directly or indirectly.

Legal Notice:

This book is copyright protected. It is only for personal use. You cannot amend, distribute, sell, use, quote or paraphrase any part, or the content within this book, without the consent of the author or publisher.

Disclaimer Notice:

Please note the information contained within this document is for educational and entertainment purposes only. All effort has been executed to present accurate, up to date, reliable, complete information. No warranties of any kind are declared or implied. Readers acknowledge that the author is not engaging in the rendering of legal, financial, medical, or professional advice. The content within this book has been derived from various sources. Please consult a licensed professional before attempting any techniques outlined in this book.

By reading this document, the reader agrees that under no circumstances is the author responsible for any losses, direct or indirect, that are incurred as a result of the use of the information contained within this document, including, but not limited to, errors, omissions, or inaccuracies.

Cover by: Angie

Introduction

For the longest time, being smart and working hard were believed to be the perfect combination for success. Anybody who was not gifted in these two areas was viewed as having gotten the shorter end of the stick. People who scored well on intelligence quotient tests, or IQ scales, were seen to have an advantage over others when it came to succeeding in life. Even today, there are cultures and societies that believe that success is mutually inclusive with being book smart. Quite frankly, there is an advantage to being book smart. You will have an easier time going through school, you are more likely to get scholarships to help you with the financial cost of higher education, and you will generally have an easier time understanding concepts, be it in school or in life.

Unfortunately, book smarts can only get you so far. After paying attention to people who excelled in school and went on to be less successful than anticipated, psychologists have determined that there is something else required in this recipe for success. This extra ingredient is referred to as emotional intelligence. Emotional intelligence is not a concept that many people paid attention to until 1995. In that year, Daniel Goleman wrote about emotional intelligence in a book that popularized the term. Before then, the term had first appeared in a research paper written by Michael Beldoch. Beldoch was a psychologist at Cornell University. Between 1964 when Beldoch coined the term and 1995 when Goleman popularized it, other psychologists had written about emotional intelligence. However, there was not much attention paid to the concept. So, what changed that made people start paying attention?

Previously, researchers had mentioned emotional intelligence and even attempted to uncover what exactly it was. However, outside of research papers, there were not many written materials available for the general public to read. Goleman's book was really the first opportunity the world had to take an inside look at the world of emotional intelligence. At the same time, Goleman had built credibility working for the *New York Times* as a science writer. The fact that he was a Harvard-trained psychologist also helped his case. Goleman's book, *Emotional Intelligence*, remained on the *New York Times* bestseller list for one and a half years, a big feat by any standards. At the end of it all, the world had a new term that continues to be explored today.

What is emotional intelligence? In the simplest terms, emotional intelligence is the ability or skill to be intelligent about emotions. This includes your own emotions and those of others. If you take into consideration the various ways that emotional intelligence has been defined over the years, you might come up with other lengthier definitions such as:

Emotional quotient or EQ, which is the other name for emotional intelligence, is the ability to recognize, discern, and manage emotions.

Emotional intelligence, often abbreviated as EI, is the capacity to be cognizant and in control of one's emotions and to express these emotions appropriately. This skill extends from controlling your emotions internally when dealing with yourself and externally in interpersonal relationships.

Emotional intelligence means being able to pay attention to your emotions and the emotions of those around you while naming or labeling these correctly and to use the emotional information gathered from this exercise to respond appropriately.

There are endless ways in which you can define emotional intelligence, but the premise of it is this: Being emotionally intelligent means being aware of your emotions and using this heightened perception to manage yourself and other people as you go about life. Sometimes referred to as emotional quotient or emotional leadership, emotional intelligence comes in handy when your IQ cannot get the job done. How so?

Human beings are emotional creatures. In the course of a single day, we go through hundreds of emotions. Examples of emotions you might experience in a day include anger, sadness, joy, fear, disgust, and happiness. While scientists have not agreed on a standard definition of emotion, it is generally accepted that emotions are a state of mind. Emotions are triggered in the brain's limbic system. The limbic system is at the base of the brain and controls emotions by triggering a reaction from the endocrine system and the nervous system. The endocrine system is everything related to hormone production, while the nervous system relates to the network of nerves in your body. Simply put, the limbic brain prompts the endocrine and nervous systems to react based on the external stimuli that you are experiencing. If you are in a state of danger, the limbic system will sense that and interpret it appropriately, prompting the endocrine system to release adrenaline.

For the most part, human beings go through the same range of emotions, albeit at varying times. While your friend may be experiencing fear at the thought of skydiving, you might be feeling intense excitement. Later on, the roles might reverse when you are about to approach your crush while your friend looks on in anticipation. There are very few humans who are incapable of feeling emotions. Psychopaths, for instance, do not experience emotions as the average person would. Studies have been undertaken to show what the root cause of this is, with some psychologists explaining that the part of the brain capable of emotions is essentially broken when it comes to psychopaths.

That aside, the truth of the matter is that you will need to manage people and the different emotions that they bring with them more often than you'll need to rattle off the names of all the countries of the world and their capital cities. Few people care whether you can name the capital city of Monaco, but a whole lot of people care about how they feel after having a conversation with you. This is not to downplay the importance of being intelligent in other matters. Indeed, knowing how to read a map, among other things, will get you places, pun intended. But at the end of the day, reading people correctly and managing your emotional interactions with them will get you even further.

This book is your go-to handbook on all matters of emotional intelligence. It explains why emotions matter in everyday situations, it identifies all the opportunities that you have to apply emotional intelligence, and it helps you to test whether you have been acting intelligently as far as emotions are concerned. This book will show you how you can learn and practice emotional intelligence, even if you have not been very good at it in the past. If you are looking to improve your relationships in the workplace or at home, this is the only book you will ever have to read. The tips and tricks included inside can be adopted for any circumstance or environment. They are easy to execute, memorable, and even fun. At the end of the book, you'll realize that there is a whole lot of fulfillment to be gained from learning how to properly manage your emotions and those of others. A happier, easier, and more successful life awaits you at the end of the final chapter of this handbook.

Chapter 1:

Why Do We Need Emotions?

Do you consider yourself to be an emotional or rational person? If you answered emotional, ask yourself if there have been times when you have wished that you weren't. Truth be told, emotions can be very messy. They can cause you to make the most irrational decisions.

Think about the last time you got really angry. What did you do? Did you end up regretting it or wishing you could take it back? You probably have regrets about the course of action you took while you were under emotional strain. You may even be tempted to think that life would be much simpler if we didn't have emotions.

But would it actually be easier? Think about it—if your life was all about logic, you probably would not have any regrets. Every decision would be carefully thought out and calculated to make sure the decision was in everyone's best interests. Relationships would not be based on love; rather, one would enter a partnership after thoroughly undertaking an evaluation, just as you would before signing a contract with a vendor in a business transaction. There would be no need for fear or sadness. You could rationalize just about anything and then go about your life without worrying about the constant presence of emotions.

It may sound perfect, but emotions do serve a purpose.

They are not just inconveniences or interruptions that we have to grapple with as we try to live our best life. Rather, emotions are an important component of survival. Put simply, emotions are the flow of information between you and external stimuli. Without emotions, you would not be able to correctly read your environment and respond appropriately. Without an appropriate response, you would struggle to overcome any environmental challenge that you might face.

Let's say, for instance, you are a fifteen-year-old minding your own business in the school hall when the resident bully comes toward you, raining taunts and blows. An expected emotional response, in this case, would be anger. When you are angry, your body goes into fight mode. This is your brain's way of protecting you. Becoming angry might save you from enduring any more taunts from this horrible human being.

Besides helping us to thrive and stay away from danger, emotions also help us communicate. Think about it—if your significant other is angry about something that you have done, you need to understand that what you did was upsetting to them. If you are a good partner, you will avoid doing that in the future out of respect for your significant other's feelings. Emotions are a part of how we speak our truth to other people and vice versa.

Emotions are also part of our identity. Are you a happy person or an angry person? You'd be surprised at how people come to define you based on the emotion you usually give out to the world. Whether this is actually who you are is a question for another day. Chances are high that you can name one or two colleagues who you consider to be happy people or angry people depending on which emotion you often catch them experiencing. Emotions thus play a significant role in how others view us.

In a bid to further understand emotion, some researchers have sought to understand the various roles played by different emotions. Typically, these researchers will focus on the more common emotions experienced by most people across the world regardless of their cultural or socioeconomic backgrounds.

The Core Emotions

The desire to understand emotions goes back to ancient times when scholars such as the Greek philosopher Aristotle put forth their own theories on the nature and purpose of emotions. Aristotle believed that emotions were an important component of moral excellence. William James, an American philosopher, and psychologist had a different view on emotion. He argued that emotions were the result of the human body undergoing various physiological changes related to the external environment.

In the period between the time of Aristotle and today, there have been several theories advanced by psychologists and scientists who have tried to explain where emotions come from and why they matter. One of the more popular theories was conceptualized by Robert Plutchik, a professor and psychologist. Plutchik came up with a wheel of emotions (known as Plutchik's wheel of emotions), which shows that there are eight primary emotions that all other emotions come from. In this wheel, contrasting emotions are mapped against each other. For instance, joy is contrasted with sadness, while surprise is juxtaposed with anticipation. The eight-core emotions included in Plutchik's wheel of emotions are the happier emotions of joy, trust, anticipation, and surprise and the less popular emotions of disgust, fear, sadness, and anger.

Why are some people more emotional than others?

If human beings experience the same type of emotions, then why do some people seem more emotional than others? Highly emotional or highly sensitive people are easy to spot. While everyone else seems to process information and emotions fleetingly, these individuals wallow in their emotions longer than is sometimes comfortable. They may cry their hearts out during sad movie scenes, open up their homes to stray animals, or become easily offended by the things people do or say, even though there was no intention to offend. At the end of the day, it is easy to think of a highly sensitive person as being overly dramatic when it comes to their actions and emotions. The truth of the matter is that this is not a cry for attention but a normal reaction based on how their brains are wired.

The study of emotions is nowhere close to being fully explored. Scientists are still in the relatively newer stages of exploring emotions and how people's genetic makeup influences them. As such, it will be a while before any consensus is reached regarding certain topics such as highly sensitive people and so on. That being said, there have been studies that have shown that how a person reacts to their environment is a result of some form of genetic conditioning.

One such study was carried out by researcher Rachael Grazioplene and her colleagues in 2012 and subsequently published in *The Journal of Child Psychology and Psychiatry*. While undertaking this research, Grazioplene and her team focused on the cholinergic system. The cholinergic system is the body system that regulates the kind of attention we give to the environment surrounding us and how we process the information we get from these environments. The results from this study showed that a particular type of receptor gene referred to as *CHRNA4* (of the cholinergic system) can influence how one turns out emotionally depending on the type of nurturing that this person receives. As such, the interaction between this gene and the environment is a major determinant in how a child will turn out. The *CHRNA4* gene is sometimes referred to as the susceptibility gene or the sensitive gene.

Think about it: If you grew up in a household where emotions are nothing to be ashamed of, you would most likely grow up believing and practicing the same. If you grew up hugging your parents and siblings, chances are high that you will also be highly affectionate with other people when you are an adult. As such, you may be born with a sensitive gene, but as long as your environment does not encourage it to flourish, you might find yourself repressing your feelings. In contrast, a person who is born with a sensitive gene and was brought up in a highly nurturing environment will have no problem being highly emotionally expressive.

At the same time, it is important to note that some people may feel the pressure to act emotionally because of what their culture expects them to be. More elaboration on the same can be found in Chapter 7, where we touch on whether women are more emotional than men.

Chapter 2:

The Personal Competencies of Emotional Intelligence

Seeing that emotions are a part of the human experience, it goes without saying that knowing how to manage your emotions is a useful life skill to have. Emotional intelligence is not a means to ignore or sweep emotions under the carpet. Emotional intelligence is also not a means of eliminating emotions. Rather, emotional intelligence calls for an acknowledgment and regulation of all the emotions of human life. And that's a whole lot of emotions considering that it has been shown that humans are capable of thousands of emotions in the course of a lifetime.

In his book, Daniel Goleman identified the five components of emotional intelligence as self-awareness, self-regulation, motivation, empathy, and social skills. If you can master these five components of emotional intelligence, you will be better placed to understand your own emotions and to relate with others.

In this chapter, we will explore the personal skills that you need to master to become more emotionally intelligent. Personal skills refer to those that must be cultivated within the self. In Chapter 3, we will further explore the social skills that make us emotionally intelligent.

The table on the next page summarizes the personal competencies and social skills of emotional intelligence.

Components of Emotional Intelligence	
Personal Competencies	Social Competencies
1. Self-Awareness Knowing yourself 2. Self-Regulation Managing your emotions 3. Motivation Motivating yourself	1. Empathy Managing other people's emotions 2. Social Skills Managing relationships

Table 1: The Components of Emotional Intelligence

Components of Emotional Intelligence: Self-Awareness

How well do you know yourself? Are you capable of describing who you are while acknowledging the internal and external experiences that you go through? Are you aware of the resources you have as a person? Why is it always so difficult to describe yourself in interview settings or on dating platforms?

Self-awareness, in the simplest terms, is an awareness of the self. The self is composed of different parts, including your abilities, thoughts, and experiences. Self-awareness as a concept has been in existence since the time of ancient civilization when a Greek philosopher summed it up as *know thyself.* Lao Tzu, a Chinese philosopher, had a lengthier view of self-awareness. He described it as such: *Knowing others is intelligence, knowing yourself is true wisdom; mastering others is strength, mastering yourself is true power.*

While these ancient philosophers were definitely onto something as far as self-awareness is concerned, it was not until 1972 that the first study on self-awareness was conducted. This study was undertaken by two psychologists: Shelly Duval and Robert Wicklund. In their study, Duval and Wicklund aimed to understand whether a person was able to pay attention to themselves or their external environment at any given moment. The end result from this research showed that an individual is able to focus internally or externally based on the circumstances. For example, at any moment in time, you may find yourself deep in thought or consciously aware of whatever is happening around you. Duval and Wicklund went on to publish a book on objective self-awareness that remains relevant even today.

In their book, Duval and Wicklund argued that self-awareness is a vital component of self-control. They stated that you can regulate your behavior to match your standards and values only if you are conscious of this behavior in the first place. In other words, if you pay attention to your emotions, you'll be better placed to understand why you feel those emotions in the first place. At the same time, if you pay attention to your habits, you are more likely to know how to manage habits as well.

For example, let's say you have a colleague at work who always somehow manages to get on your last nerve. You have yet to understand why this is the case because you never take the time to analyze why you always react negatively to their presence. But after reading this book and understanding how self-awareness works, you decide to take some time off for introspection. You realize that this colleague always has something negative to say about other people's weight. You further realize that you are touchy about this topic because your weight, while no longer an issue now, was a constant issue when you were growing up. You are now able to pinpoint why every interaction you have with said colleague always feels like an attack on you. You are also better placed to regulate your actions and behavior toward your colleague.

For instance, you may choose to stay away from this particular person, or you might even try and explain to them why talking about other people's weight is offensive. Of course, the colleague will also need to learn about self-awareness so that they can understand which topics are fodder for conversation and which ones are not. Chances are high that this colleague is not even remotely aware of their actions and their impact on others, and for as long as they remain unaware, they will continue to offend others. This lack of awareness stems from the fact that they are not aware of their own self and how they interact with themselves and the environment around them.

How self-aware are you? Here are a few questions that you can answer to see how self-aware you are:

1.   Have you ever watched yourself in a mirror while engaging in an activity such as eating?

2.   If a person you know well criticizes you, how does it make you feel? Do you feel angry, disappointed, or are you more curious to understand why they feel that way about you?

3.   Would you describe yourself as a jealous partner? If yes, are you obsessively jealous, or do you consider your jealousy to be within the bounds of reason?

4. Are you the type of person who likes to have someone to blame when something goes wrong, or do you just go with the flow and chalk it up to bad luck or other unforeseen circumstances?

5. When participating in sports or any other competitive activity, have you ever felt the need to or actually thrown a tantrum?

6. Do you consider yourself sympathetic toward others? Have you ever been accused of not being sympathetic enough?

7. Are you able to read other people's moods?

8. How likely are you to take your frustration out on another person?

9. Do you consider yourself a highly sensitive person?

10. Do you hold firmly to your beliefs about politics and religion, or do you leave room for flexibility?

These are just some of the questions that you can use to gauge your overall self-awareness. No doubt by the fifth question, you will start to see a pattern forming if you answer the questions truthfully. People who lack self-awareness have a higher likelihood of looking outside of themselves for reasons to justify their behavior. They are often unable to rein in their emotions, and they prefer to place the blame on someone else. The signs that distinguish a person who is not self-aware from the rest of the bunch are very clear for all to see.

Characteristics of People Who Are Not Self-aware

They are bullies.

In the fight to put an end to bullying in schools, kids have been reminded over and over again that bullying is a form of cowardice. Indeed, bullies are cowards. A tragic fact that confronts adults many years after leaving the playground is the fact that bullies do not go away; instead, they grow up. There are adult bullies, and they coexist in the same spaces that we do. They attend the same churches that we do; they work in our workplaces, and they love the same bands as us.

The behavior of a bully stems from the fact that they are scared about something, but instead of confronting the source of their fear, they prefer to scare another person. Bullies exhibit a stark lack of self-awareness in that they channel their energy toward the wrong thing. If you are constantly bullying others, you may lack self-awareness and need to look inside yourself to determine what it is that you are scared of.

They are highly controlling.

To be fair, most of us like to be in control of various aspects of our lives. In fact, you should never allow your life to hurtle out of control if you can do something about it. Unfortunately for many individuals who are not self-aware, the desire for control is all-consuming and one that extends even into other people's lives.

Why is this so? As human beings, we often struggle with various things in our lives that do not always go according to plan. When a person who is not self-aware is met by a situation that seems uncontrollable, they try to make up for it by choosing to control other things. For instance, a person who is failing at their job might try to run their home with an iron fist. If this person was self-aware, they'd realize where their need for control stems from and then take steps to direct their attention appropriately.

They prefer to be passive-aggressive.

However, much of a people-person an individual may be, there comes a time when having an uncomfortable conversation is inevitable. We are human beings who come from different genetic backgrounds and sociocultural environments, and so once in a while, we are bound to clash in one way or another. When this happens, the sensible thing to do is sit down and talk it out so that the event does not recur.

Unfortunately, people who are not self-aware do not see it this way. They have a deep-set dislike for encounters that require facing issues head-on and choose passive-aggression as their go-to problem-solving mechanism. In being passive-aggressive, these individuals are able to keep the mask on and seethe on the inside because they are afraid of confronting what is hidden deep within themselves. The problem with being passive-aggressive is that it is often emotionally draining, and it never solves the problem at hand. It leaves one party feeling used and abused and leaves plenty of room for miscommunication.

They have a whole lot of made-up reasons that do not involve being accountable.

When you have a severe lack of self-awareness, it follows that you will never be able to acknowledge the events in your life that you are responsible for. Instead, you will go through life needing to place the blame on a third party. If you are late to work, you will blame the traffic, not the fact that you woke up thirty minutes late because you stayed up late the previous night. Individuals who always have an excuse or two to cover their tracks have yet to learn the art of introspection. Yes, life happens, and things do go unexpectedly from time to time. However, as individuals, we are sometimes responsible for why things happen. When this is the case, it doesn't hurt to hold yourself accountable. In fact, this is a measure of maturity and self-awareness and will earn you the respect of people around you.

They suffer from delusions of grandeur.

There are some people who believe that they are so good at their art only to fail miserably when it is time to share the said art with an audience and/or judge. You may have seen them on popular talent shows such as American Idol, Britain's Got Talent and such like. You have probably judged them from the comfort of your couch while wondering how they thought they could sing/dance/put on a magic show when they obviously have no talent. You may have even gone so far as to wonder why their friends or family never told them that they are irredeemably terrible at singing/dancing.

The truth of the matter is this: You cannot save a person from their own delusions of grandeur if they are not self-aware. While delusions of grandeur have been shown to occur more extensively in people who suffer from mental illness, they are also present in non-patients. Believing yourself to be more impressive than you actually are is a great boost for the self-esteem and something that we could all benefit from time to time. However, there exists a healthy limit, at which point you go from self-confident to outright delusional. Self-awareness helps to curb this delusion. Self-awareness balances out the self-image you have so that while you know you are good-looking, you remain aware that you are not the most attractive person in the world.

Ways to Improve Your Self-Awareness

A great thing about self-awareness is that you can practice it and improve regardless of how self-aware you are today. You can go from being totally oblivious to being the most self-aware you have been in years. By using tried and tested tactics that you can apply in your everyday life, you can completely change how you see yourself internally and externally.

Observe yourself

The first thing you'll need to do is become an observer of yourself and your life. You have to remain an objective and neutral observer, though. You cannot judge yourself while you are doing this observation. If you are judgmental, you will not be able to pick up the important points and notes along the way. You must ensure that you are only taking notes about the things happening in your life—the emotions you are feeling and the thoughts you are thinking in the course of a day—while fighting the need to insert a remark here or there.

For instance, let's say you've just run into your office crush in the office kitchen. You exchange pleasantries, and then because you are nervous, you proceed to babble about something that did not need to be said. Take note of this moment and the feelings you are experiencing. It is tempting to try and dismiss this as a stupid and cringeworthy moment that you do not wish to revisit. But doing so will only make you susceptible to repeating the same encounter, which is exactly what you are trying to avoid. However embarrassing a situation is, you'll want to take note of it and then revisit it later for a full understanding of the same.

If you are not sure, you can remember everything that happened to you during the day, feel free to keep a journal. A journal comes in handy because you can always refer to it when you need to think about how you were feeling even after several days have passed.

Set aside time for introspection.

After collecting enough mental notes, it is time to get started on the analysis process. This is likely to happen at the end of the day while you are just about to go to bed. This timing is best because you are done dealing with the world for the day, and you can be honest with yourself in the comfort of your home. The soul-searching that will happen at the end of the day will be your opportunity to identify why you have acted as you did during the day.

Why did you snap at your colleague right before lunchtime? What were you angry about? Why did you call your ex, whom you had sworn never to call? Why did calling him to make you feel so lonely and worthless? There is always a reason and a root cause for anything that happens under the sun. If you are able to identify the root cause for all your thoughts and emotions, you are well on your way to becoming more self-aware. And you know what you can do with roots? You can uproot them if they are not the kind you want to keep feeding.

Ask your friends and colleagues to tell you what they really think about you.

Trusted friends can be helpful when it comes to an understanding of how others see us. Ask your close friends to describe you in the most honest, non-hurtful way that they can. This informal feedback will give you insights on how you come across and how you relate to others.

It could be that you have always thought of yourself as a nice person only to find out that your friends think you are a bully. When this happens, do not take offense. Rather, you should see this as an opportunity to become a better person. If it is possible, enlist your friends in helping you identify instances when you act like a bully. This way, you will gain a better understanding of the instances where you tend to act intimidatingly in an uncalled-for manner without being aware that you are coming across as a bully.

The feedback you receive at your workplace can also be very useful in helping you become a self-aware person. Most companies have employee feedback mechanisms that allow a person to get feedback from their juniors, peers, and bosses. Instead of getting mad at the type of feedback you receive, consider taking the time to understand why people are saying those things about you. True, one vindictive person may anonymously leave hurtful feedback, but an opinion that is shared by more than two people might be worth a second look.

Shift your mindset.

When people say it's all in mind, you better believe it really is. In the introduction, we explored emotions, and the role played by the brain in their formation. The brain is at the center of all emotions, and as such, it is safe to say that it is all in mind. If you can rewire your brain, you can help yourself experience emotions that are positive and beneficial to your human experience.

For instance, scientists say that every time you hold back your anger and, instead of lashing out, opt for a more peaceful option such as walking away, you are training your brain to help you become a calmer person. This is something that you can easily try even at home. What's the one thing that really gets you mad? Slow internet connection? Next time your provider slashes your speed, do not resort to your default reaction of lashing out and throwing things at your computer. Instead, simply get up and go for a quick walk around the neighborhood. Try this a couple of times. By the third time, you will no longer feel a need to be angry about slow internet speeds. In any case, what's the worst thing that could happen if you lose your connection for a couple of minutes? Yes, the world will transmit several terabytes of data without your contribution, but it could be worse, right?

Shifting your mindset also means aligning your feelings and thoughts with your value system. Many times, we do things because it is what has always been expected of us. Being clear about what you value as a person will lead to a much-needed paradigm shift that will be a big step toward self-awareness.

Forgive yourself.

We are good at extending grace and forgiveness to others when they need it, but we're not so good at doing the same for ourselves. At one point or another, you will come to the realization that some of the beliefs you have held or the things you have clung onto as unquestionable truths were not that. This is something that might happen after periods of introspection and conversations with others.

When you arrive at this point, you must shed all judgment and resentment that you feel toward yourself and forgive yourself wholeheartedly. This means you also have to forgive yourself for the silly thoughts, actions, and feelings that you might find yourself in during the course of your day. Remember the awkward way you acted in front of your office crush? You must forgive yourself for that too. It is part of the learning process.

Start anew.

With the new awareness of your feelings and thoughts and a hard look at the value system that influences them, you can now get started on beginning anew as a self-aware person. Self-awareness is not a one-and-done job. There are many times when you will forget and go back to the old and familiar. That's the thing about human beings; we love to return to the familiar because it feels comforting. However, tempting it might be to want to go back to your comfort zone, you must remember that change is often painful and uncomfortable. Being self-aware might seem and feel like a daunting process, but it is exactly what you need to become exactly who you were meant to be while forming meaningful and respectful relationships with those around you. You might have to confront some personal demons along the way, but the outcome will be worth the effort.

Practice meditation and mindfulness.

Many people go about life while awake and on autopilot. Very few get to experience the mindfulness that comes with being in touch with your innermost self. To achieve this, you will need to practice meditation and mindful awareness.

Mindful awareness is a term that is used to refer to the heightened consciousness that comes with being in touch with your thoughts, emotions, sensations, and experiences during every waking moment of your life. Mindfulness is exactly how you will be able to take note of your experiences during the day, allowing you to have material to mull over later on.

Mindfulness also allows you to be in control of your life. It means the difference between going through life and experiencing life. In one, you are a pawn that is tossed here and there at the mercy of your emotions; in the other, you are the queen calling the shots.

There are various meditation apps available on both Google PlayStore and Apple's App Store to help you learn how to be more mindful as you go about life. A key trick to being mindful and staying calm is to always stay conscious of your breathing and to try and process how you are feeling internally before projecting this onto your external environment.

Components of Emotional Intelligence: Self-Regulation

As an adult, you can do pretty much anything you want without needing to ask for permission. You can decide to not show up for work. You can opt to have ice cream for dinner, and cake can be breakfast if you so wish. If you don't feel like having a healthy meal, you can have all the pizza you can afford.

If this is the case, then why are adults not running amok trying to outdo each other as far as crazy, unconventional breakfasts and dinners are concerned? The reason is that many adults have a skill known as self-regulation. Self-regulation knows that while you might have impulses to do exciting things, it is always better to choose the option that is more aligned to your long-term goals. A self-regulation is a form of self-control that has a long-term perspective.

In the course of your adult life, there will be moments when you wake up, and the last thing you want to do is get dressed for work. However, you will also know that there are bills that need to be paid and goals that need to be met. Perhaps you are aiming for a bonus or promotion, or maybe you want to be part of an award-winning team at work. Either way, putting this into perspective will help you get dressed and show up regardless of your earlier impulse to quit and be done with it.

There are two main types of self-regulation: behavioral and emotional self-regulation. Behavioral self-regulation involves regulating your own behavior and acting in a way that fulfills your best long-term interests. An example of behavioral self-regulation is what was mentioned above when you feel like quitting but show up anyway. Behavioral self-regulation enables you to feel one way but acts differently because acting this way serves your best interests.

Emotional self-regulation, on the other hand, involves the regulation of emotions. As we saw earlier at the beginning of this book, we are all emotional creatures. However, we do not always have to be at the mercy of our emotions. It is possible to exercise control over your emotions so that you do not put yourself in jeopardy.

Let's say, for instance, you are in a heated meeting with your boss. He is the type of boss that is domineering and condescending and will throw his employees under the bus without hesitation. Your boss proceeds to launch an unwarranted attack on you and the entire team that you lead. You can feel the anger rising within you. You look calm on the surface, but you are seething underneath. You are ready to give your boss a piece of your mind. Then, you take a deep breath and calm yourself down. Anger will not get the job done, you remind yourself. Anger, in this case, is a useless emotion. If you get angry, you will only be allowing your boss to have a go at you and possibly turn your name in for insubordination. Instead of getting angry, you calm yourself down and try and look for the valid points that you can work with. You just won at emotional self-regulation.

Emotional self-regulation is crucial because it allows us to rein in our emotions before they take control of us. Here's the thing: You will not always be able to control how you feel about something, but you can control how you handle those feelings. There are certain steps that you can take to ensure that you get better at self-regulation.

Define your personal values.

The very first thing that you must do is ensure that you are clear on what your values are. Our values are what keep us grounded. When everything else gets foggy and blurry, your values will be the lighthouse guiding you to the shore. As such, start by identifying what you hold near and dear as your core values.

As an individual, you will have many values throughout the course of your life. Some will fall by the wayside as you grow older, while others will withstand the test of time. It is your responsibility to keep defining what your personal code of ethics is because this code will help you make decisions that are beneficial to you. When conflicted, you can always refer to your values and act appropriately. Having the right kind of values is one of the simplest ways to self-regulate because you do not even have to think too much about decisions. You just have to checkboxes and walk away from the things that do not meet those values.

Take responsibility for your actions.

Here's the thing: You can only self-regulate if you first hold yourself accountable for the actions you take. As long as an action remains someone else's fault, you do not have any control over what that person does. However, if you admit to yourself that you are the reason for the things that go wrong in your life, you can take steps to ensure that you no longer act in conflict with your best interests.

Let's say, for instance, you wake up on a Saturday with the worst hangover of your life. You went out the previous night at the invitation of a friend and stayed up all night drinking and partying. For as long as you keep blaming your friend for the hangover, you will always wake up on Saturdays feeling as if you got run over by a truck. However, once you realize that it was your choice to accept or decline the invitation in the very same way that it was your choice to drink yourself senseless or not, you will begin to see that you can choose better for yourself. However convenient it would be to think otherwise, the truth of the matter is that we are rarely innocent bystanders who run into misfortune. Ninety percent of the time, our actions and choices determine what happens to us.

Make calm and collected your go-to mood.

Some people seem to be better at staying calm than others. How do they do it? The ability to stay calm when everything and everyone else is falling apart is something that is learned over time. You need not wait until someone is on your last nerve to practice staying calm. You can make it a habit to be a calm person regardless of the circumstances surrounding your life.

There are certain habits you can include in your life to help you become calmer in your decisions and interactions. These include getting enough sleep, trying out new things that help you put personal matters into perspective, keeping a gratitude journal, and even going for relaxing walks. Even if you do not have the time for all this, you can still become calmer by using what you have within you. The body knows how to handle stress on its own. All you need to do is breathe deeply and feel the air move through your nose and all the way to your lungs. A few deep breaths will have you feeling much better and calmer whenever you find yourself starting to feel agitated.

Components of Emotional Intelligence: Motivation

Motivation is the driving force that causes you to do something that is beneficial for you in the long-run. Different people are motivated by different things, including money, fame, or even power. If you are looking to lose some extra pounds, for example, you are motivated to keep going to the gym by the body that awaits you at the completion of your weight loss journey. If you are a student, the promise of a good career and a well-paying job may be exactly why you keep showing up for your classes even when you do not feel like you are up to it. While motivation shows up in different forms, its components are standard across the board.

The first component of motivation is the activation of a process. This is the part where you decide that you need to get something done and thus take the first step. This could range from enrolling in a class to signing up for volunteer opportunities to downloading that dating app that your friends are all using.

The second component of motivation is persistence. Here's the thing: The hardest things to do often require the most motivation. Think about it. You do not need a lot of motivation to keep ordering your favorite pizza, but you do need motivation in heaps to commit to eating healthy. As such, persistence is the sign that you are ready and committed for the long haul, regardless of how tough the going gets.

Lastly, there is an intensity component of motivation. When you are determined to get something, you will pursue it with all the energy that you can muster. You will not make excuses, and you will not cut corners or try to get yourself out of what you signed up for. This is what intensity is all about. In a college setting, for example, a student that understands the intensity aspect of motivation knows that studying is a regular activity and not something that they do when finals are just around the corner.

So, how does being motivated as a person make you more emotionally intelligent? When you are fueled from within, you are more likely to pursue the things that fulfill you and make you happy. Motivated people have been shown to be both more positive in their outlook and very adaptable to change. They are generally nicer to be around and make good team players. A motivated individual looks forward in the direction of their dreams and goals and exudes a certain air of confidence and positivity wherever they go. Motivated people are also more assertive in the pursuit of their goals and will not say yes to every request that comes their way. They understand how to deal with the people who may want to stand in the way of their goals. They also know how to identify the people who will, later on, become assets in the pursuit of their dreams.

Let's contrast this with an unmotivated person. What is such a person likely to do?

An unmotivated individual is exactly the kind of person that you do not want around you by virtue of their negative outlook on everything. Unmotivated people like to see the glass as half empty all the time; they like to blame others and will often not carry their own weight. An unmotivated person has not marshaled their internal resources for their own good and cannot do the same for other people.

It has been said that charity begins at home, and this is definitely something that people who lack motivation do not seem to grasp. A person can only bring the energy they feel inside to their external world. If you are a shriveled raisin lying on the sidewalk on the inside, you cannot be a blooming sunflower on the outside.

Do you consider yourself highly motivated or highly lacking in motivation? If you feel like you could use a nudge in the right direction, consider doing the following to boost your overall morale about life:

1.   Set yourself some goals that excite you.

2.   If there's a goal that you need to set that does not sound particularly exciting, figure out something about it that is of interest to you. For instance, if you need to do well in math but aren't exactly fond of math, think about how having good grades will help you achieve another goal that is exciting, e.g., going to college.

3.   Write your goals down so that they look real. If possible, make a vision board. Written down goals are a constant reminder of the things you want to achieve at the end of a particular period of time.

4.   Put in place a reward system that allows you to give yourself a reward every time you hit a milestone in your goals.

5.   If you have a big goal, break it down into manageable bits so that you do not feel overwhelmed.

6.   Find someone to support you on your journey to achieve your goals. It might be your mentor, a trusted friend, a family member, or your favorite colleague. Going it alone is fine, but having a companion along the way ensures you have someone to hold you accountable and to lift you up when you find yourself slumping.

Chapter 3:

The Social Competencies of Emotional Intelligence

Emotional intelligence includes how you relate to yourself and how you relate to others. In the previous chapter, we looked at the personal competencies that make up emotional intelligence. These are the skills that you need to develop internally as a person so that you become a self-aware person who is motivated to become better every day.

Besides working on yourself internally, you must also manage how you relate to others in your everyday social interactions. This is where the social aspect of emotional intelligence comes in. It has been said that no man is an island, and you most likely have a community around you that you interact with. It is important to ensure that you are interacting with this community in a manner that is emotionally intelligent. If this is not the case, you might find yourself with a rather unpalatable label, and who wants those? It is not especially flattering to know that everyone thinks of you as a clueless jerk.

In this chapter, we will focus on empathy and social skills—the last two components of emotional intelligence that are intended to take you from clueless jerk to social butterfly.

Components of Emotional Intelligence: Empathy

Empathy, not to be confused with sympathy, is what you feel when you put yourself in another person's shoes. In contrast, sympathy is basically a pity that has been dressed up. When you are empathetic toward a person, you feel their pain and their thoughts. If they are going through a crisis, you go through the crisis yourself. Empathy is the more committed version of sympathy, and this might explain why a lot of people do not have the time for it. Empathy calls for time and patience. It is not simply throwing a pity-party for someone and then going on your merry way. Empathy demands that you stick around and look for a solution that can reduce that person's suffering because their suffering is your suffering as well. Quite often, people use sympathy and empathy interchangeably. Based on our earlier definition, this is both incorrect and misleading. Let's take a look at some examples of sympathy versus empathy.

Sympathy	Empathy
You run into a friend who has been trying to lose weight for the longest time. She looks drained and overwhelmed. You have never struggled with your weight, but you do understand that weight loss can be a tough journey, and you let her know as much.	Your friend later runs into another friend who has tried to lose weight and succeeded. This friend lets your friend know that they truly know and understand what they have been going through because they went through the same thing. The second friend is able to relate and connect with your friend's struggles because they have gone through the same experience.
Your friend's mother has been diagnosed with cancer. Your friend is devastated. As an only child, she is extremely close to her mom. Over a period of about a year, you watch as she struggles to keep up with work demands while being the sole caregiver for her mother. As your friend's mother's life ebbs away, you cannot help but feel deep sympathy for both of them.	Your other best friend has gone through the pain of losing their parent to cancer. They understand exactly what your friend is currently going through. They can relate to the angst of not knowing how they will go on without their main cheerleader. They know first-hand the devastation that comes from watching someone you dearly love crumble under the weight of a terminal illness.

Your boss, who is also a well-respected businessman, makes a bad investment and loses all his money. This new development necessitates he files for bankruptcy. When you receive this news, you think to yourself, "Wow, it must be really difficult to be in such a situation." While you understand that losing all your money must be painful, you really have not gone through it yourself and can only offer your sympathy.	Your boss's friends have made bad business decisions before. Some have even come to the brink of bankruptcy and almost lost their families because of it. They are empathetic to your boss's plight as they truly know, understand, and can relate to the overwhelming emotions that come with losing all your money and investments.

Table 2: Differences between sympathy and empathy.

The table above is an illustration of sympathy versus empathy in real life. However, it is important to note that you need not have gone through a person's exact circumstances to be empathetic. Instead, you can train yourself to view things from other people's perspectives so that you can become more empathetic. For instance, you need not have lost a pet to understand and feel the pain of a pet owner who has gone through the same. If this were the case, then empathy would be something that is exclusive to only a select few who have gone through suffering and life-altering events. Instead, empathy is something that you can train yourself in and get better at.

Empathy is very complicated, so it goes without saying that it is a skill that requires serious honing. A lot of the people who believe themselves to be empathetic are really just sympathetic.

The good news is that you can learn how to be better at putting yourself in other people's shoes. A person who masters empathy is well ahead of others when it comes to forming better interpersonal relationships.

But first, some interesting facts about empathy:

1.   The term empathy has Greek origins. It is derived from the Greek term for physical affection, which is *empatheia*.

2.   The Greek term was first adopted by two German philosophers and turned into a German word (*Einfühlung,* which means *'feeling into')* that was later translated to *empathy* by an English psychologist.

With that out of the way, let's get into the details of empathy. How many types are there? What can you do to improve it? Why is it that some people seem more empathetic than others? Is it genetic or a result of social conditioning? Really, there are seemingly endless questions about empathy, most of which we will answer here.

Types of Empathy

While empathy is defined as being able to connect and relate to another person and their suffering, it is more than just that one thing. It is actually three things, and there are three different types of empathy. The difference lies in the part of the brain that drives the empathy. The three types of empathy include cognitive empathy, social empathy (sometimes referred to as emotional or affective empathy), and empathetic concern.

Cognitive Empathy

Cognitive is an adjective that comes from the noun *cognition,* which refers to the process of acquiring information and then processing it through thought and your overall senses. Cognition may also be referred to as perception, reasoning, or insight. From this definition of cognition, it becomes easier to guess what cognitive empathy is all about.

Cognitive empathy is essentially the practice of seeing things from other people's perspectives. Instead of simply processing the information we have from our own perspective, cognitive empathy calls for us to look at that information as if we saw it through someone else's eyes.

Our perspectives are shaped by different factors. We are born with some of these factors, while others are a result of our upbringing and the environments we find ourselves in. Common influencers on perspective include your age, race, gender, nationality, experiences, needs, and even your natural talents, just to name a few. The fact that there are billions of permutations that can be derived from these factors means that all seven billion plus of us in this world have very different perspectives on things. Cognitive empathy calls for us to try and see the world through the perspectives of the people we interact with instead of trying to force our own perceptions and discernment on them.

Cognitive empathy looks like this:

Your friend calls you in the middle of the day while crying hysterically. She has just been fired unceremoniously from the job that she has had for the last five years. She cannot believe her bad luck and is terrified at being jobless again after having gotten used to a regular paycheck and what she had previously believed to be job security. In the back of your mind, you have always thought that this job was wrong for her. It is a desk job, whereas she is the creative type that prefers to be adventurous and flexible. She has complained about the job since the beginning, and her only motivation to stay on was the fact that the job helped her pay her bills. While she cries and laments her situation, you are tempted to tell her that this is a good thing because she is out of a workplace she has hated from the very beginning.

Instead of doing that, however, you will help yourself to look at this job loss from your friend's perspective: It is the loss of a regular paycheck that had come at the worst of times when she was planning to buy a house and possibly start a family. She will now have to start looking for another job and probably even start over in a different part of town or the country.

Instead of blurting out the first thing that comes to your mind, you stand back and acknowledge that this is indeed a big change that came at the worst of times. You let your friend know as much and allow her the space to feel angry and disappointed without imposing your contrary views on her. In doing so, your friend feels understood and knows that she has at least one ally in the world. If you had opted for the option of showing your friend the other perspective (yours), you would have made a person that is struggling with a major disruption feel misunderstood and alone when all she wanted to be a friend whose shoulder she could lean on.

Cognitive empathy does not always come easily to the majority of people. A lot of the time, people tend to be stubborn about their perspectives and unwilling to see things from any other angle. Others will immediately jump into Mr. Fix-It mode without first acknowledging that the other party just wants to be understood.

Emotional Empathy

Emotional empathy is the ability to share another person's feelings. Emotional empathy, which also goes by the name affective or primitive empathy, is often unconscious. For example, if you watch a sad movie scene, you are likely to find yourself in tears. You did not will yourself to cry—it just happened. As a matter of fact, there is a scientific explanation about why people cry during movies and what this has to do with empathy.

During the highly emotional scenes of a film, your body is likely to release higher amounts of oxytocin. Oxytocin is a hormone that is sometimes referred to as the *love hormone* in that it makes us care for others. Under the influence of oxytocin, you become more empathetic and are therefore likely to cry during a sad movie scene even though you know that it is all made up. Of course, studies on how oxytocin and empathy correlate are still in their formative stages, and we will only know for sure what goes on behind the scenes once these studies are completed.

Empathetic Concern

The empathetic concern is a type of empathy that involves feeling the pain and suffering of others and working toward alleviating it. The empathetic concern is being able to acknowledge the distress of another person while also stepping in with a solution that will help them be free of the distress. The empathetic concern is also referred to as compassionate empathy and is a type of empathy that has been exercised by millions of people who step in to help in times of crises such as earthquakes, hurricanes, tornadoes, and so on.

The empathetic concern is often the best kind of empathy because it not only involves showing compassion for another person's suffering but also stepping in to make sure they do not have to suffer anymore. A lot of times, the people who need empathy the most are not just looking to be understood or to have someone cry along with them. Instead, they wish for someone who could help them get out of the suffering that they are in, and this is where the empathetic concern comes in. If you are in a leadership position, the empathetic concern will be your best bet as far as building better working relations with your juniors or your team.

That being said, it is important to note that the different types of empathy do not occur in distinct stages in your life. There will be many times when you will experience all three types of empathy at the same time, especially if you are the kind of person that would be described as naturally empathetic. When you are experiencing all types of empathy at once, it is important to be conscious of, which is the most beneficial for the moment.

A doctor, for instance, will do no good by displaying too much emotional empathy. Think about it—the last thing you need as you are getting wheeled into the operating room is to catch your surgeon in tears. Yes, it is heartwarming to know that your surgeon is able to relate to your pain, but what you need more is their empathetic concern as they work toward making sure that they'll fix whatever is wrong with you.

How to Develop Empathy in Your Everyday Life

Here's the thing, you are either an empathetic person, or you're not. You cannot switch empathy off or on whenever you feel like it. You also cannot refer to that one time when you were empathetic in 2009 and then try to pass yourself as a person that is full of empathy. In order to be considered empathetic, you must commit to the skill in your everyday life in the same way that a person needs to tell the truth on more than one occasion before they can be considered truthful.

Lucky for you, becoming more empathetic is actually pretty easy. The biggest obstacle you will face on your journey toward empathy is yourself. Why? Because nine out of ten times, human beings tend to be self-absorbed. Empathy calls for you to leave some room in your life for other people and their thoughts and feelings. Here are some practical tips that you can apply in your life to get better at empathy:

Tip #1: Listen more than you talk

A Greek philosopher named Epictetus summarized the importance of listening more than talking like this: *We have two ears and one mouth so that we can listen twice as much as we speak.* Unfortunately, the world today is such that everybody is talking, and nobody seems to be listening. As long as you are talking, you will never really be able to tell what the other person is thinking or feeling. It is important to take a pause and let other people talk because that is the main avenue through which thoughts, perspectives, and emotions can be communicated.

The best kind of listening is what is referred to as active listening. In other words, you must listen in a way that shows you are invested in the conversation. Sitting across from your conversation partner without saying a single word or while staring at them, blankly will only make them feel uncomfortable and uncared for.

Active listening is pretty easy to achieve. The first thing you will need to do is put away all distractions aside. This means that you should not check your phone for Facebook updates while your friend or colleague is pouring their heart out to you. Checking your phone or doing other things while your friend is trying to have a heart-to-heart conversation with you is incredibly rude and in poor taste. Instead, put away all distractions and focus your attention on the person speaking. Steady eye contact lets them know that they are important and that you are paying attention.

Now, you do not want to get all creepy with your eye contact to the extent where the other person begins to feel as if you are staring. A clever way to maintain appropriate eye contact is to lock eyes for five seconds and then look away. During this time, you should not be staring but rather gazing at them softly and with compassion.

However ridiculous the story might be, never roll your eyes at a person who is opening up to you about something. Remember, they are feeling those emotions and thinking those thoughts because the experience was valid to them. Even if you believe crying over a dead goldfish is being overly dramatic, do not let these thoughts show on your face.

At the same time, you want to ensure that your active listening is peppered with just the right type of insightful questions. Ask open-ended and non-judgmental questions that help them draw out the root cause of their troubles. The idea of active listening is to stimulate the other party to arrive at a solution of their own making. All along, the other party will believe you solved their issue when, in fact, you just listened and gave them a platform to rant and bounce off the solutions they already had in their mind.

Let's say, for instance, your friend comes to you complaining about their partner. They have been together for two years, and your friend is starting to feel as though she might not be the right partner for him based on how she has been behaving.

Friend: I don't know, it just feels as though she is taking me for granted.

You: Why do you say so?

Friend: Just the other day, I came home early and cleaned the house and did the laundry just so that she could relax and enjoy our date night. She cannot enjoy a date night as long as the unfinished household duties are at the back of her mind. And you know what she said?

You: What did she say?

Friend: Nothing. Absolutely nothing. She did not even act as if she had noticed all the hard work I put into it.

You: Have you considered talking to her about it?

Friend: No. Not really. Do I have to?

You: It would help to get her perspective. What do you think her perspective is?

Friend: Well, she does the same household duties, and I do not exactly hold a parade for her. I guess she did not see the big deal about me helping.

You: ...

Friend: Oh yes, that's probably it. Why is it a big deal when I do it and not a big deal when she does it? I should probably check the social conditioning I have received on the expected gender roles in society.

You: Yes, like the fact that dads are parents too and not babysitters.

Friend: Ha-ha, exactly!

The whole point of this conversation is to show you that you can flow with your partner without imposing your beliefs and perspectives on them and still allowing them to get as much as they want off their chest. Sooner or later, they will get to their a-ha moment where they solve their problem and go on their merry way. The fact of the matter is that you will get the credit for the solution, and they will leave believing that you are the epitome of empathy.

Tip #2: Allow yourself to be vulnerable

Being vulnerable is scary. Allowing other people to see the most sensitive parts of you can feel like making yourself a sitting duck. However, it is important that other people see you for the human being that you are. We are all flawed in our different ways, and we have our own fears and flaws. We feel things, and we worry too. When someone is brave enough to be vulnerable with you, do yourself a favor and allow yourself to show that side of you that you would rather not show under any other circumstances. Self-disclosure is not intended to take away attention from the other party. Rather, it is a means of creating mutual understanding and making the other person feel that you understand what they are going through.

Let's say, for instance, your friend comes to you with marriage troubles. They have run into tough times with their spouse after using up the graces of the honeymoon period. They are confused and cannot figure out what they need to do to fix things. One way of being vulnerable with them is letting them know that you also experienced the same phrase when you got married. You are not trying to speak ill of your spouse or marriage, rather you are letting your friend know that it is human to go through what they are going through. After this disclosure, your friend will feel more connected to you and more trusting of what you have to say regarding their little problem.

Tip #3: Put your assumptions and judgments aside

We all have preconceived notions about things that are based on our own experiences and understanding of issues. When a friend is lamenting their misfortune, it can be tempting to rush to what we think we know in an effort to give them some comfort. Unfortunately, doing so is often a problem rather than a solution. As difficult as it may be, it is crucial that you put all your assumptions and judgments aside and focus on seeing the world as your friend sees it. Empathy is the patient. It is not something that is rushed so that you can move on to the next person who needs it. Many times, empathy requires that you shut up about what you know and allow the other person to tell you what they know or think they know.

You will not always interact with people who share your world views. You might even have friends who believe in the most ridiculous things. Regardless, you must always be prepared to try and understand where they are coming from, instead of trying to change who they are.

Tip #4: Use your imagination

Chances are high that you will need to be empathetic toward people who are going through experiences that you have never gone through. In such instances, how are you expected to be empathetic? It's simple, really. You just have to use your imagination. You do not need to have gone through labor to know that childbirth can be a very painful experience. You only need to imagine how excruciating it must be to use your body to bring forth a human being into the world.

You can fire up your imagination through reading and also by allowing your mind enough space to roam uninhibited. Your mind can take you on adventures that no airplane can, so whenever possible, let it guide you. Of course, if you have not experienced something, do not use your imagination to lie to others. A man who uses his imagination to tell a woman in labor that he went through the same thing five years before is an outright liar. And you know what does not go well with empathy? Lies. Lies do not quite fit into the same space as empathy.

Tip #5: Tune into the welfare and needs of others

Empathy is not something you throw at others when you wake up in the morning or when you show up at work. For there to be empathy, there has to be something that hinders the well-being of another person. You cannot empathize with another person simply because they exist. You can, however, empathize with another person about the heartbreak or hardship that they are going through.

Every human being has what they prioritize as their major needs outside of the universal basic needs. When these needs are not met, a person might consider themselves to be undergoing suffering. For example, if you have a need to be loved (and most people do), getting dumped by a significant other can induce a whole lot of suffering.

When you are comforting someone in this state, you must approach it from the point of view of their needs. Even if you think the person who dumped your friend/colleague is not exactly a catch, you have to keep these thoughts to yourself and then look at it from the perspective of your friend's welfare. Being attuned to people's welfare is especially critical in empathetic concern because it is only by knowing what is missing from someone's life that you can be able to replace it.

Components of Emotional Intelligence: Social Skills

The term social skills is a rather sweeping term that is used to refer to all the skills that you use or need to use when relating to people. In the context of emotional intelligence, the definition of social skills is narrower. The social skills that you need in order to become more emotionally intelligent include communication and persuasion skills, conflict management skills, and even leadership skills. You also need to become great at building rapport and collaborating within teams. These are the skills you'll especially need to work on, particularly for your job. But even in personal relationships, knowing how to manage your social interactions goes a long way in cementing friendships and romantic relationships. Let's take a look at each of the social skills mentioned.

Persuasion skills

Persuasion is the art of convincing or influencing someone to do a particular thing that they would probably not have done had you not intervened. (Persuasion is not to be confused with its more eerie cousin by the name of manipulation.) Whether you hold a leadership position or not, it is necessary to learn how to influence people to do the things that you need them to do. Before you can influence anybody, it is important to read them correctly so that you understand what appeals to them. The skill of persuasion is one that has been used by salesmen all over the world to convince customers that they need to buy a particular product.

Communication skills

The way you say the things you say is critical. Good communication skills are the difference between conveying a message with clarity and getting your message lost in the wording. Good communicators tend to be alike in their characteristics. They know that communication is not just about talking but listening as well. They pay attention to verbal and nonverbal cues as well, both their own and those of their audience.

Good communicators are confident and friendly and communicate respectfully. They can express their opinions without necessarily forcing them on others. If you consider yourself challenged in the area of communication, you can take classes and do lots of practice to get better. Paying attention to how your favorite public speaker or mentor carries themselves when speaking will also help you pick up the important communication skills that you need to be learning.

Leadership skills

You're probably wondering why leadership skills are a part of emotional intelligence and not a consequence. The truth is that leadership skills, and emotional intelligence are interlinked in a manner such that the division between the two becomes blurred. It is difficult to say where leadership skills start and where emotional intelligence ends.

Think about your favorite leader. It could be your boss, a business person, or even a political figure. How well do they relate to other people? If they relate incredibly well with others, would you call this emotional intelligence or leadership skills? Natural-born leaders have the ability to read others and appeal to them. At the same time, because they have this innate capacity for emotional intelligence, they come across as good leaders.

Good leaders are also usually self-aware and often highly motivated.

If you do not consider yourself a natural-born leader, you can still work on your leadership skills by honing your emotional intelligence competencies. More often than not, you will find that people will prefer to put empathetic people who are self-aware, self-regulating, and motivated in leadership positions. Working on yourself first will get you where you need to be as far as leadership is concerned.

Conflict-management skills

What is your go-to move when faced with conflict? Is it to run and hide, or is it to address the conflict head-on? Quite frankly, most people would rather do without conflict. Yes, there are a few human beings who thrive in the midst of conflict, but this cannot be said for many people. Whether you love conflict or hate it, chances are high that one day you will find yourself standing in the middle of it. When this happens, you must know how to manage the conflict.

A good conflict manager knows how to handle a problem without victimizing any parties involved in the conflict. Rather, they let the involved parties understand that the objective is to find the solution rather than apportion blame. In work and personal relationships, conflict management is a crucial skill to have. It allows you to navigate the landmines that come with differing perspectives and interests without getting blown into pieces. Good conflict management calls for tact and diplomacy.

Winston Churchill defined tact as the ability to tell someone to go to hell while making them look forward to the trip. This really does sum up everything that you need to know about how to handle conflict should it arise in your life. It is not really about getting everyone everything they demand; it is more about getting everyone to a place where they believe their grievances have been heard and resolved.

Chapter 4:

Understanding Emotional Drain and Energy Vampires

Up until this point, we have made one significant assumption in this book: that you are surrounded by emotionally mature and decent people in your life who are solely motivated by the desire to take advantage of you. The nature of emotional intelligence, especially the empathy component, is such that you will be giving a whole lot of you to others. You will be investing your emotions in an effort to gain an understanding of other people's feelings. You will also be investing your time in trying to appreciate other people's thoughts. What happens when you start to feel drained? What causes you to start feeling drained in the first place?

Have you ever spent some time with someone only to leave their company feeling extremely drained? Or maybe you have dated a partner who seemed to enjoy leaving you depleted of all your emotional resources. It might also be that you work with colleagues that leave you feeling worse for wear at the end of every workday. The emotional drain manifests itself in various ways. It is the effect of being under too much stress, both mentally and emotionally. The emotional drain might look like boredom, irritation, sadness, and even anxiety. Whatever it may look like, emotional drain is a very serious problem. Going through long periods of emotional drain sometimes has tragic consequences in the end.

So, what exactly causes an emotional drain? The shortest answer is this: energy vampires. Energy vampires, also known as emotional vampires, are individuals who sap the energy out of other people. The main motivator for energy vampires is their own emotional immaturity. Unfortunately for you, a lot of people tend to be emotionally immature. This means you are at a very high risk of encountering an energy vampire.

How does being emotionally immature make one an energy vampire? When a person is emotionally mature, they know how to handle their emotions because they are well-equipped to deal with them. Emotionally immature people are not similarly equipped and, thus, they deal with their emotions by bringing other people into their drama. Often, the inability to handle emotions goes back to some trauma experienced in childhood.

For instance, children who are neglected in their childhood often grow up to be adults who have a myriad of issues, including low self-esteem, anger problems, and even an inability to define their true identity. When this is the case, the adult might lash out from the pain they have carried all their life. They might now even know they are doing this because they experienced pain. Sometimes, the trauma lingers in the body long after the years have passed. The brain recognizes this pain and may not pinpoint the exact time that it happened. The brain just knows that the body is experiencing this pain. Therapy is often the bridge between the brain and the body as far as understanding this trauma and where it comes from. As such, it might not be someone's intention to be an energy vampire, but they'll be one all the same because of what they have gone through.

At the same time, there are individuals who sap the energy out of you, knowingly and intentionally. Such individuals include psychopaths, who are known to lack empathy, and narcissists.

Many times, when a person is dealing with an emotional vampire, it can be hard to admit what is happening. As human beings, there is some guilt and shame that comes with admitting that a particular person drains every last ounce of energy from you. You might feel as if saying that makes you a bad person. When the individual in question is a relative or loved one, you might become very conflicted between what you know and how you feel. It is, therefore, important to know the very clear signs of the emotional drain so that you can move onto the next step of deciding how to deal with an emotional vampire.

Signs of Emotional Drain

Besides feeling exhausted after an interaction with someone, there are numerous other signs that can point to a problem. Unfortunately, many of these signs can be attributed to other things, which explains why they might go unnoticed for a long time. For instance, if you are having trouble sleeping, you might think it is because you are stressed about tomorrow's presentation. The real cause might actually be the fact that you are in an emotionally draining relationship with an energy vampire. This brings us to the first sign of emotional drain, which is insomnia.

Insomnia

You'd think that the brain would know to fall asleep when you are emotionally depleted to allow you the chance for some required rest, but this is not the case. The emotional drain is often accompanied by stress, which is characterized by a racing mind that is trying to contain a million and one thoughts. When your mind is in this state, it can be very difficult to quiet down for a night of relaxing sleep. If you are having trouble sleeping, and have not undergone a major life event that would explain your insomnia, you might want to look around at the people you spend your time with. One of them might be sapping all the joy and life from you, leaving you with nothing to look forward to at the end of the night.

Lack of Motivation

In Chapter 2, we looked at motivation and the role that it plays in our lives. We said that motivation is the force behind the go-getter attitude that allows us to achieve our long-term goals, even if it means putting up with the hard work of the present. To be a highly motivated individual, you must be at a good place mentally.

When you are down in the dumps, you lack the necessary emotional resources to motivate yourself. The things you used to love are no longer appealing, and you have to give yourself a pep talk before getting out of bed in the morning. Energy vampires have a way of stealing all the resources from you.

An energy vampire might come in the form of a boss who is always criticizing your work unfairly, even when you have delivered pure gold. You will likely not have the mental or emotional energy to get into it with such a boss or even the job itself after several months of constant criticism. While you had previously enjoyed your job, you will likely catch yourself, not wanting to show up at the office.

Hopelessness

Hope is a thing that has been channeled by many a person to get themselves through difficult situations in life. When a person is without hope, they see no end to their suffering. They believe that what they are going through is permanent and that every day they live through will be worse than the previous. Hope is powerful, and the absence of it is also powerful, albeit with the opposite effect. Martin Luther King, Jr., said this about hope: *Everything that is done in this world is done by hope.* So how can you expect to do anything when you have no hope?

Energy vampires who are intentional in their emotional abuse are especially good at sucking out all the hope from your life. A narcissist, for instance, might make you feel as if you are the most worthless person in the world and that you'll never be able to achieve anything. When you get such a review from a person that you love, it is easy to lose any hope that you had for the future.

It is critical that you never allow any person to take your hope away from you. Hope is what you'd be left with if all your material and earthly possessions were to be taken away. Hope is what drives you to rebuild when the rug is pulled out from under your feet. Protect your hope at all costs. Do not allow anybody to get anywhere near your hope.

Detachment

When you have been emotionally abused and kicked around for a long time, you become numb as a defense mechanism. You no longer experience emotions like other people. Instead, you are immune to emotions of joy and happiness. You are used to pain, and so you prefer to prepare your brain and body for it. You might not even be conscious of this process. You may just find yourself one day wondering when was the last time that you had a good laugh.

Constant Crying

Why do we cry? We cry when we are happy, sad, shocked, surprised, scared—this much we know. What we might not know is the science behind crying. Fortunately for us, though, some scientists already took it upon themselves to understand tears, what causes them, and what role they play. Whenever you are experiencing strong emotions, your limbic system communicates the same to the autonomic nervous system, which in turn activates your tear glands resulting in a good cry. This is why some people might cry during happy moments—their limbic system simply sensed the rush of emotion and sent that all-important message to the nervous system.

Now, when you are emotionally drained, you are dealing with many strong emotions all at once. As such, you will find yourself crying even when you did not mean to. In itself, crying is not a bad thing. In fact, it is okay to cry your heart out whenever you feel like doing it. What's more, tears contain a natural painkiller which would explain why some people report feeling better after having a good cry. However, if you find that you are crying more frequently than is the norm, and at the slightest provocation, you might want to think about the most recent events of your life. It could be that you have been spending time with someone who makes you feel really bad about yourself, or maybe you have constantly been fighting with your spouse. Either way, something is up, and you need to look into it.

Irritability

When you are emotionally drained, all your emotional and mental reserves are depleted to the extent where you no longer have any patience for anybody. You may find yourself being intolerant of the smallest things. Someone could be chewing loudly next to you, and you'll be fighting back the urge to punch them in the face. Previously, you were able to ignore this blatant lack of table manners without a second thought. There is a clear correlation between stress and anger, and it is one that you can easily notice even without the help of a psychologist. Think about it: When you do find yourself snapping most at the people around you—may be your partner or even children? Chances are high that you are less fun to be around when you are stressed about things.

How to Deal with Energy Vampires

As noted, energy vampires are all around us. You can also be an energy vampire depending on the circumstances in your life. For instance, there are times in your life when you might be extremely needy and codependent, depending on what you are going through. If you have ever needed someone to fill an empty space or need in your life, you probably were an energy vampire at that moment.

Seeing that we all have the capacity to be energy vampires, is there any need to learn how to deal with it? Would it not be easier to just let ourselves exist in our natural states as well-meaning but somewhat needy people who sometimes suck the soul out of others without intending to? Well, unfortunately, there are those vampires that will leave a trail of emotionally drained people in their wake without feeling any bit of remorse about it. An energy vampire of that kind can do a whole lot of destruction, which is why it is important to know how to deal with the intentional and calculating emotional vampire.

The very first thing that you need to do when dealing with an energy vampire is to recognize them for who they are. A lot of times, we are involved with the wrong people for a long period of time before realizing what exactly they are and the damage they cause in our lives. If the feeling you get after spending time with someone is constantly negative, consider this a red flag that you want. As human beings, we tend to extend a whole lot of grace and forgiveness to people who do not deserve any of those things.

We say, perhaps they were having a bad day or perhaps they are dealing with tough things in their life. We make excuses for people when deep down, we know that they are bad for us and that they are indeed not having a bad day. If someone constantly behaves like a jerk, they are probably a jerk. Do not allow such a person to keep getting away with it just because you feel gracious toward them.

A crucial thing that you will need to learn when dealing with energy vampires is how to ground yourself. Grounding yourself involves knowing who you are, understanding yourself, and remaining true to who you are so that you are not easily swayed by people who come in and out of your life. It is vital that you have a clear and solid understanding of your individuality and your energy. Energy vampires have a way of identifying vulnerable people that they can take advantage of. Vulnerable people include those who are easily influenced. For example, if you are easily rattled by what people think and say about you, you will become the perfect fodder for emotional vampires.

Think of yourself as a sturdy oak with your soul's roots stretching deep into the earth. Come storm or sunshine, this oak perseveres. Be the oak. Let the energy vampires tire themselves out while they try to figure out how to uproot you.

Remember to always protect your personal space at all times. Personal space acts as a barrier between us and the world around us. Protecting your personal space means being careful with who you allow into your life. If you make it easy for an energy vampire to intrude into your personal space, you will be setting yourself up for a whole lot of heartache and emotional drain. While it is a nice thing to be friendly to the people you come across, it is not your obligation to be friends with everyone. You must properly vet the inner circle that comes close to your personal space.

Imagine sitting across an energy vampire for an hour while they suck your very soul out of you. Draining, right? However, if you sit across this same vampire while you are in a group of people, their negative energy is spread across the three or four of you. If you absolutely must deal with an energy vampire, consider doing so while in a group setting so that you can protect some of your energy.

If your boss is an energy vampire, for instance, do not allow yourself to be lured into one-on-one working lunch. Instead, opt for group lunches where the entire team gets to tag along. Of course, sometimes this may be out of your control, considering the fact that your boss might prefer to impose his opinion on you without asking for yours in return. That being said, you can always get creative and ensure that you do not allow yourself to get into conversations that leave you feeling physically drained and mentally exhausted.

Everyone has topics that they feel strongly about. Avoid the energy vampire's trigger topics if you want to spare yourself the negativity. For instance, you may have a friend that loves to be negative about work. They cannot stop talking about how much they hate their work and how much their boss hates them. Every time you have a discussion about work with your said friend, it leaves you feeling worse for the wear. Once you realize that work is the triggering topic for this friend, lay off conversations regarding work indefinitely. Go for topics that they are less likely to start complaining about. You can direct the conversations in your life in the way that you like so that you are not drained by your conversation partner.

Lastly, remember that you do not have to deal with an energy vampire. It is absolutely within your rights and freedom as a human being to refuse to deal with someone who is bad for you. Do not ever feel as though it is your job to be patient with someone or to fix someone who is broken. You are trying to live your best life, and you cannot spread yourself thin, trying to save everyone else. However, compassionate you may be, it is important to recognize that some of the deep-set issues that people have can only be addressed with the help of a professional. It is fine to walk away from someone who ruins your mojo. It is fine to tell a person you have just started dating that you do not see the two of you working out. It is okay to choose self-preservation. You can never be everybody's savior.

Types of Energy Vampire

Last but not least, it is important to note that energy vampires come in different shapes and sizes. While they all have the same result of draining someone of their energy, they implement their devious ways differently. Here are the noteworthy energy vampires that you should be on the lookout for:

The Forever Victim

Some people just love being the victim in every story. They play the role perfectly and use every opportunity to let the world know how unfair life is to them. If you have such a person in your life, you will quickly get tired of hearing them whine about everything and anything. They whine when the boss requires that they do the job they were hired to do. They complain when they face a minor inconvenience. They complain when you do not pick their calls because you were at a meeting, and they'll even complain after you pick up their call because they think your tone is harsh or unfriendly, or whatever they want it to be for that occasion. If you think reading about the things a person with a victim mentality will complain about makes you feel exhausted, imagine what the actual complaining does to a person who has to deal with such an energy vampire. It can be truly energy-depleting. Long after you have left the company of such an energy vampire, you will still hear their whiny little voice ringing in your ears.

The It's-All-About-Me Vampire AKA the Narcissist

Imagine living your life with someone who absolutely does not consider you a person worthy of empathy or any other sort of consideration. This is what a narcissistic energy vampire is all about. To them, the world revolves around them. If they sneeze, you must run immediately to them and see if they are about to catch a cold. God forbid that is the case because now you have to shelve your life and ensure they recover by administering tender, loving care that they themselves would not be willing to spare if the roles were reversed. A narcissist vampire will make you feel as if you were born to do their bidding. They will steal all your sense of empowerment and leave you feeling deflated and worse for wear. Even when they sense you are getting overwhelmed, such vampires never quit. They take and take and take until there is nothing left of you to take.

The Intimidator

It is a matter of the fact that weakness is louder than strength, the Intimidator is an energy vampire that is lacking in strength. As such, they compensate by trying to act tough and strong when, in fact, they are quivering in their boots beneath the surface. The Intimidator is an emotional vampire that likes to dominate each and every space they are in, regardless of the circumstances or the occasion. They talk the loudest in the room, are often inappropriate, like to push people around, and will have no hesitation spewing hate when they know they can hide being something. You will often find a lot of intimidators hiding behind computer screens and spewing their hate and bigotry about everything and anything. Intimidators often find strength in numbers (of their own kind) because they know they lack the innate strength to act alone. Intimidators do not care for other people's points of view—only their opinions matter. An energy vampire of the sort makes for a very bad boss because they get drunk on power and believe they are more powerful and crucial to the organization than they truly are.

The Drama-Loving Energy Vampire

Some people tend to drag drama everywhere they go. They carry it with them to personal relationships, to workplaces, to restaurants, to schools, and to just about anywhere they go as long as there is an audience. The melodramatic energy vampire thrives in chaos because it fills the empty space in their life. Chaos also enables them to get the attention that they so love.

If you are dating the overdramatic energy vampire, you will know it even before anybody tells you. They will pick fights about the smallest things. They will be offended by everything. They will come home from work, talking about how everybody hates them. They will throw tantrums and even throw things. Everything with the melodramatic vampire happens on a level that is several decibels louder than the level of a normal human being.

Do not stick around, thinking this one will change. Often, the overdramatic energy vampire never changes. They just evolve into something else, sometimes a worse version of themselves. For instance, if they had previously solved fights by throwing things around at home, they might escalate to showing up to your workplace to pick a bone. If you can spot the drama signs from a mile off, run for your life. Do not take their bait. It never works out well.

The Judgy Vampire

Have you ever spent time with someone who was highly critical of almost everyone they came across? Judgmental people are all around us, and they are impossible to please. They like to pick people apart and put them back together in a manner that will never allow them to be whole again. They are always armed with snide remarks that they throw around. Nobody is good enough for them.

The reason they look at the world this way is that they really do not like themselves. They are often highly insecure and believe they are not good enough. As such, they project this low self-worth to other people. If you are already struggling with your self-esteem, a judgmental vampire will take what's left and crush

71

it to smithereens. Judgmental people can learn to be better human beings and less energy-sapping by getting the professional help that they obviously need. Before then, they remain as the energy vampires that they are. There are no prizes for guessing how unpopular these vampires are.

The Unknowing Vampire

Sometimes, vampires are not even aware of the fact that they are vampires. Vampires are not always the characters described above who are easy to pick out in a crowd. Vampires can exist in the form of human beings who have grown to depend on you too much. Children, for instance, can be really energy-sapping. Mothers all over the world can attest to this. Even the nicest people in the world can steal your energy if they become highly reliant on you. The unknowing or innocent vampire can be dangerous in that you might not even know they are one until you are completely drained of your emotional resources.

Take a look around your life and think about the people you pour yourself into on a daily basis, either from a sense of duty or because you love them. How does this constant pouring affect you as a person? Do you go to bed feeling utterly exhausted because you had to cater to these people all day since waking up? If yes, then you need to devise a means of encouraging the unknowing vampires in your life to be more self-sufficient. Once they carry some of their weight, then you will be able to recharge and save some energy for yourself.

What to Do When You Are the Vampire

You've probably gone through this chapter and identified instances where you have been an energy vampire yourself. Or maybe it's more than just a few instances. Maybe you have realized that you have been an energy vampire for as long as you can remember. Now you are probably feeling guilty about all the energy you sapped out of people when you did not mean to. Or maybe you are still in denial about it and feel like it's more of leaning on people and ranting than stealing their energy.

As you work through your self-awareness (see Chapter 2 for more details), you will start to notice things that you were previously ignorant about. You will see patterns of behavior that are self-serving and destructive to others. You will acknowledge instances when you have acted unfairly toward others. You will identify opportunities that you had to be better and, unfortunately, lost. It will be quite an eye-opener for you. Whatever it is that you unearth, you must acknowledge this without being too hard on yourself. We are prone to error from time to time by virtue of being perfectly imperfect and flawed human beings. When you are unaware of something, then you are bound to mess up and act selfishly and hurt others along the way. Forgive yourself and hold yourself accountable for your future actions, seeing that ignorance will no longer be the reason for your behavior.

At the same time, realize that other human beings do not exist to be taken advantage of or to serve you. Other people are going through things that they need help with. Stop to help them more often than you stop using them. Imagine how incredible the world around us would be if we stopped to help more often than we stop to complain or lament. Everyone would be filling up everyone else's energy reservoirs. We would all have full tanks of positive energy to drive us wherever we wanted to go. It sounds very *kumbaya* when you put it that way, but it is possible. The world around you does not have to include the entire population of the state that you live in. The world around you could simply be the loved ones that you share your home with. A wise person once said that anybody who wishes to change the world must first go home and love their family. It does not get more profound than that.

Make a habit of pouring yourself into the people you love more than you take out from them. Be kind to your spouse. Instead of complaining about things that happened at work during lunch break, consider having a nice dinner date to make up for it. Only you can determine the kind of energy that you will have in your life. Go for the good energy. Let all the negative energy know without any doubt that you have no room for it in your life.

Chapter 5:

Emotional Intelligence at Work

Ever since the world started paying more attention to emotional intelligence, thanks to Goleman, there has been a segment of society that has been particularly engrossed in understanding what EQ can do for them. That segment is the business world or the corporate workplace. C-suite executives and hiring managers all over the world are keen to reap the benefits of emotional intelligence. Since the 1990s, there has been plenty of research to support the claims that emotional intelligence makes a person a better employee.

The baby boomers of the world did not care much for emotional intelligence in the workplace. They simply did their jobs, collected their paychecks, and went home. Today's workplace has changed. Millennials want more from their jobs than a mere paycheck.

Robert Walters, a recruitment company based in the United Kingdom, undertook a survey of millennials that sought to understand various aspects of their jobs and professions. From this survey, the recruitment company was able to determine that millennials are motivated by things that are totally different from what motivated the generations before them. Millennials are not content to settle for a job for the sake of having a job. Rather, they want a job that gives them a bigger purpose. They want to feel that they are fulfilled and growing. They want to feel like they are part of a bigger community.

The millennial workforce also wants the freedom to plan their workdays without feeling as though they are under a microscope. They want to be able to be social in the workplace. They want a life outside of work, otherwise referred to as work/life balance. They also want to be rewarded for the things they do through pay increases, promotions, and recognition.

When compared to the older generations, it is clear that millennials have set quite a high bar. It is no wonder that hiring managers have sleepless nights trying to determine who is the best fit for their company. Against this dynamic backdrop, it goes without saying that hiring decisions can no longer be influenced by IQ only. While hiring managers still want to hire smart candidates, they are being swayed more and more by emotional intelligence. In fact, in one survey carried out by Harris Interact for Career Builder, 75 percent of hiring managers said that they would rather hire an employee that is emotionally intelligent than one who has a high IQ. This is not to mean that hiring managers all over the world are united in downplaying book smarts. Rather, it shows that companies have finally come around to the fact that it takes more than knowing about the knowledge contained in books to survive in the workplace of today.

Importance of Emotional Intelligence in the Workplace

Emotional intelligence in the workplace is not just a fad that people are excited about that will go away after a while. There are true benefits to hiring an emotionally intelligent workforce.

Emotionally intelligent employees handle pressure better.

Just as the workforce of today is different from the workforce of yesteryear, the workplace has also changed. Before, workplaces tended to be more relaxed. The modern workplace looks to be more cutthroat and pressure-filled. With this in mind, hiring managers know that emotionally intelligent employees will be better placed to thrive in an environment of pressure. This is because they are able to manage their emotions even when the going gets tough. Imagine an environment where employees are unable to manage their emotions. What is likely to happen when a critical deadline is coming up? Probably lots of yelling and scapegoating. This would definitely be a recipe for disaster.

Emotionally intelligent employees are better decision-makers.

Decision-making is an everyday activity in the business world. You need to make decisions about how to solve client problems, which clients to pitch to, which colleagues to include in particular teams, how to format a report for a client, how to manage your workload efficiently, and a myriad of other decisions. The more emotionally intelligent you are, the more capable you are of making good decisions. When you know how to manage your emotions, you are able to make decisions that are not simply emotional. Emotions are good and all, but they don't usually make for very good catalysts in decision-making.

Let's say, for instance, that you are a team leader working to deliver a project for a client. There is one colleague that is very good at performing financial due diligence, a skill that you need for this project. Unfortunately, this colleague does not really like you, for reasons best known to them. They have made this clear to the extent of being publicly disrespectful. What do you do?

A person that is lacking in emotional intelligence might be tempted to engage in a power struggle with this colleague. After all, the colleague should respect the team leader regardless of their differences.

However, if you are emotionally intelligent, you will devise a way to deal with the colleague because you realize that getting into it with them is only going to ruin the progress of the team. You will figure out a way to play the role of a team leader without giving them an arsenal that they can use against you. Instead of playing their game, you will kill them with kindness. You will be fully invested in being the bigger person, and you will not allow a said colleague to drag you to their level. This is because you are self-aware, self-regulating, motivated from the inside, and well equipped with the social skills needed to handle a colleague that is behaving like a petulant child.

Employees with high EQ handle conflicts better.

The workplace is a convergence of many personalities. When different personalities meet in one place, there is a high likelihood of crashing. Colleagues will not always get along. You may have potlucks or staff parties every other weekend, and there still will be differences and conflicts between the employees. In the face of conflict, you need employees that can resolve their differences with as little drama as possible.

High EQ employees are more motivated.

Let's say you are a business owner who has worked hard to build your brand and hire a reasonable number of people to work for you. You invested your life savings into starting a company because you believed in your vision and mission. Two years after hiring your employees, you start to notice that all of them are coming in late, dragging their feet in their delivery to your clients, and sometimes not even showing up for work. Your brand starts to decline. Your clients are no longer satisfied. You feel defeated. Where did you go wrong?

You hired employees who were not emotionally intelligent.

As we saw in Chapter 2, intrinsic motivation is a measure and component of emotional intelligence. Companies that hire emotionally intelligent people do not have to constantly remind them to be motivated. These employees are already motivated on their own and do not need the extra push.

Emotionally intelligent employees respond better to criticism.

Imagine having an employee that sulks every time they are criticized for something. How annoying would that be? As an employer, you do not have the energy or time to deal with employees who view feedback as a personal attack. Employees who are emotionally intelligent understand that there will be moments when they need to be corrected. Their self-identity and sense of worth are not pegged on what their boss has to say about them. They are secure in themselves and accepting of feedback, both negative and positive.

Outside of regular employees, workplaces also benefit from hiring emotionally intelligent managers. Such managers are better able to manage teams, communicate the vision of the company, and even resolve conflict. A manager that is low in EQ might cause the downfall of the company that they work for. Such a manager will try to impose their authority on the rest of the employees using intimidation, threats, and other unwarranted tactics. The same goes for C-suite executives and anybody else that is in a management position at the workplace.

How Do Hiring Managers Determine a Candidate's Emotional Intelligence?

If hiring managers are seeking to hire candidates with high emotional intelligence, the question that naturally follows is this: How are they able to tell who is high in EQ and who isn't? Do they give a test? Are they silently judging you without your knowledge? It's more of the latter, but instead of judgment, it's more of an observation. You can tell a lot about a person without asking them direct questions.

Hiring managers will know if you are emotionally intelligent by checking how you have worked with teams in your previous roles. They will want to know how well you got along with these teams and whether you held any leadership positions in your past. Be sure to mention any leadership positions that you are or were responsible for during interviews. Do not downplay the very important role this little fact plays in determining how the hiring manager sees you.

If you have been to an interview in the recent past, you were probably asked about a challenge that you faced and how you tackled it. Human resource divisions do not ask this question for the sake of entertainment or to fill space. Rather, they want to understand what approach you take when faced with challenges. Do you run and take cover, or do you face challenges head-on with equal parts courage and creativity? The answer to this question could very possibly mean the difference between being hired or receiving that infamous regret letter.

The other popular question that hiring managers love to ask is: *What is your biggest weakness?* This leaves many candidates to feel the need to lie that aiming for perfection is their biggest weakness. This answer has been given so many times in interview rooms that recruitment teams have grown to anticipate it and possibly roll their eyes whenever they hear it. Now, whether you are the perfectionist you claim to be or not, the whole point HR is asking is because they want to know if you are self-aware. You need not lie about your weak points; you only need to demonstrate that you know what those points are. Of course, you also do not want to shoot yourself in the foot in order to demonstrate how self-aware you are. Saying that you often oversleep and arrive late for work is exactly how you do not get hired for the job.

Chapter 6:

Emotional Intelligence at Home

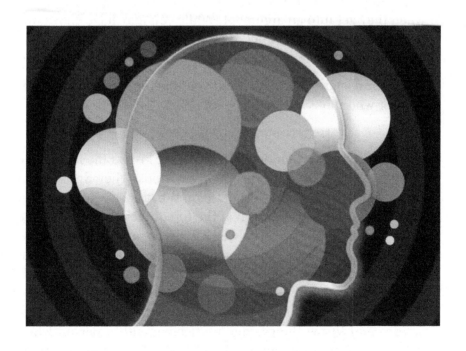

People who are not emotionally intelligent tend to make for terrible partners in a relationship. Granted, emotional intelligence is not the be-all and end-all of a relationship, but it is a pretty big deal. You really do not want to be intimately involved with a person who is not emotionally intelligent because they will always fall short of your expectations, at least where emotions are concerned.

Dating a person with a low EQ can be really frustrating. It can stop you from enjoying all the comforts and benefits that come with a relationship. A partner with a low EQ can also do a lot of damage to your self-esteem. Unfortunately, many people do not know how to tell whether their partner or any other loved one has a low EQ. You may have heard your friend complain that her boyfriend is never attuned to her feelings or that he always yells when they get into an argument. While you may have known that this is wrong, you probably did not understand the relationship between such behavior and low emotional intelligence.

Here are signs that should tell you that you are dealing with a partner who ranks low on the emotional intelligence scale:

1.   He is controlled by his emotions.

A person that is emotionally intelligent knows the importance of always being in control of their emotions. They do not allow their emotions to get the best of them. What does your partner do when you argue? Do they yell at the top of their voice, or do they calmly share their point of view? It is normal to feel agitated when the person you love is confronting you about something. But all things considered, it is never okay to become disrespectful in the form of yelling or name-calling. If your partner argues calmly, they are emotionally intelligent. If they like to shout and scream and throw things, you are dealing with a person who is severely lacking in emotional intelligence. If they get angry but know it's better to walk away than to yell, then you can keep dating them. The fact that they know it is wise to distance themselves from a volatile conversation says that they are a better person than the one who stays and yells.

2.   He is not able to read your feelings.

Imagine dating someone who is never able to tell how you are feeling. Sounds frustrating, right? While we do not mind readers, we are at least supposed to somewhat be able to read the emotions of our significant others. Being able to understand verbal and nonverbal cues shared by your partner is a sign of emotional intelligence. If you have to spell out each and every emotion that you are feeling to your partner, you are definitely dating someone who needs a whole lot of practice on EQ. Of course, your partner cannot be expected to sense your every emotion and anticipate your every need. That is a lot to ask from one person. However, they should at least be in tune with your reality. If you are crying in the darkness of your bedroom, it does not require a rocket scientist's assessment to tell that you are sad.

3.   He has no network of friends/acquaintances.

Emotionally intelligent people make friends easily because they know how to relate to people, how to make people feel listened to and understood, and how to maintain healthy relationships. If your partner just moved into town, it's okay for them to not have friends. However, if he has been living in the same neighborhood for five years and he still does not anybody that likes him enough to stick around as a friend, then you might just have caught yourself a fish that is lacking in EQ.

4.   He is incapable of sympathizing or empathizing with anyone.

Empathy is an important component of emotional intelligence. If your partner has trouble being sympathetic or empathetic toward you and other people, you have a big problem on your hands. Lack of empathy is a sure-fire sign of low emotional intelligence. Worst case scenario, lack of empathy is also one of the indications that someone is a potential psychopath.

5.   He behaves inappropriately.

There's always that one guy (usually an uncle) at a wedding who tells the most inappropriate jokes while everyone else cringes in their seats. What do you do when you find yourself involved romantically with this sort of person? You'll probably call them aside and tell them that they were highly offensive earlier when they gave that toast. Chances are high that you'll approach this conversation while walking on eggshells because you are used to their emotional outbursts.

The inability to read a room is a major giveaway that someone is not emotionally intelligent. The fact that a person can stand in a room full of people and keep telling jokes that make everyone uncomfortable shows that they are incapable of reading nonverbal cues and cannot pick up on the emotions or mood of the people in the room. It can be quite embarrassing to be on the other side of such a relationship.

6.   He is often the loudest person in the room.

Now, there's nothing wrong with being extroverted. In fact, it is a good thing that extroverts exist because they fill the awkward silences that introverts leave in their wake. However, if the person you are dating is loud in a manner that is obnoxious, then you likely have a person that is emotionally immature on your hands. An outgoing person that is emotionally intelligent knows that extraversion does not mean talking over others or talking non-stop without allowing other people to get a word in. Remember that the ability to communicate powerfully without needing to raise your voice is a measure of emotional intelligence. It follows, therefore, that a person who is unable to talk without shouting is extremely low on emotional intelligence.

Dealing With a Partner Who Has Low Emotional Intelligence

What do you with a partner who is driving you nuts with their lack of emotional intelligence? Do you toss them out the door, or do you give them a chance to get better? Logistically, it is easier to just do away with people of low emotional intelligence. However, we all know that the heart wants what the heart wants. Besides, if you were to remove all the low EQ people from your life, you'd probably be left with only one or two people. Yes, high EQ is not very prevalent. Which brings us to the tips on how to deal with someone who you love but who sometimes makes you want to claw your eyes out.

Tip #1: Address the elephant in the room early on.

When two lovebirds meet for the very first time, they want the other to think that they are perfect little angels who can do no wrong. They go on dates, make each other laugh, and say only those things which are flattering. When one of them does something wrong, like a snap at a poor waiter who's only trying to do his job, the other smitten lovebird looks away and chalks it up to a stressful day. Even when this recurs at a different restaurant, the lovebird is willing to forgive and forget. At least, that happens until it finally happens in the safe confines of their loving house. Then, the lovebird realizes that there is no way one person can have seven bad days in a row unless they are the cause of the bad days.

You are the lovebird in the story, and the moral of the story is that you need to call out bad behavior whenever you see it, especially when you see it more than once. True, your partner is allowed to have one sulky day when he does not want to talk to anybody, but five days is stretching it. How are you going to have a relationship with someone who cannot articulate their feelings? If something bothers you about your partner (especially something that indicates low EQ), bring it up. Do not allow it to fester and leave you reeling in resentment. Couples who communicate openly in a relationship stand a better chance of staying together longer anyway.

Tip #2: Watch your tone.

So, you've taken a few emotional intelligence quizzes (including the one in Chapter 8 of this book) and have figured out that you are obviously better at emotional intelligence than your partner. What next? Do you lord it over them? Do you make them feel like a teeny tiny person because they struggle with their emotions? Absolutely not. Because if you do that, then it means the tests were inaccurate. Therapists have said again and again that the way a couple speaks to each other really influences how long they stay together.

Some people score poorly in EQ not because they want to but because they do not know better. Your role as an emotionally intelligent partner or spouse is to bring your partner to the other side. The side where people speak respectfully and with empathy. The side where people are good listeners who do not interrupt others while they are talking. Being condescending about your superior emotional intelligence is only going to make your partner resentful of you. Remember, your partner is probably not even aware of the fact that they lack in emotional intelligence (refer to the self-awareness section in Chapter 2). Do not make things harder for them by patronizing them.

Tip #3: Be realistic about your expectations

You've been suspecting that your partner has low EQ all along, and this book has cemented this suspicion by providing you with solid evidence of what EQ is and what it is not. Now what? Should you share this book with your partner and demand that they read it from cover to cover and report back to you in a week's time, complete with a higher EQ?

Absolutely not. That is not how it works.

Yes, there are some aspects of emotional intelligence that you can practice and get good at in just days. For example, you can aim to be a good listener by always allowing the other person to finish talking before you respond. This is a tactic that can be implemented in a matter of days. However, learning how to be in tune with emotions, how to be a better communicator, and how to care for others might take a bit more time. Your partner might not even be up for it. They might fight you when you suggest that they should try doing this or that. Remember that low EQ people tend to hate change. Converting your partner will not be a walk in the park. However, if your partner truly loves you and is committed to your relationship, then you can help them get started on the baby steps that they need to take for the relationship to become even more fulfilling than it really is.

Tip #4: Remember, it's okay to fight.

Every relationship has its own fights. There can never be a relationship without fights unless the parties are afraid to share their true opinions. Fights strengthen relationships. They give a platform for partners to share the feelings that they have kept hidden deep within. Whether you are fighting about EQ-related matters or any other thing, do not feel any guilt or shame over it. Even the most emotionally intelligent people fight with their loved ones. They just know better than to yell or name-call or hit.

As long as you are fighting without tearing each other down, you are on the right track.

Tip #5: Let the other person choose to change.

It's true that you can influence another person into changing by modeling the kind of behavior that is appropriate. However, you can never force a person that does not want to change to change. Change is such a personal decision that must be made by an individual when they are ready for it. If your spouse behaves in a particular manner that you find to be emotionally immature, they have to get to a place where they see it from your perspective, and then decide to change. This might take a whole lot of time and may even seem impossible at first. Sitting around, waiting for them to be ready might take up all your patience. Only you will be in a position to decide whether they are worth the wait or not.

Tip #6: Sometimes, you'll have to walk away.

Let's say you have been dealing with a partner for a long time who obviously has very low EQ. This partner is not in tune with your feelings; they openly disrespect you, have no qualms about yelling, are always dramatic about something, and cannot seem to see what the problem is. When you try to talk to your partner about these issues, you are met with cold treatment. What do you do?

At some point, you have to pull the plug on a relationship that is not working. Relationships are not recyclable plastics that you can keep and use for another purpose when you are done using them for what they were originally intended. A relationship is supposed to be positive addition in your life. If your partner is exhibiting signs of low or nonexistent emotional intelligence, including being emotionally abusive, it is well within your right to walk away. In fact, you should not only walk but run as fast as your high EQ heels can carry you. Somewhere out, there is someone who is self-aware and motivated that is bound to appreciate a respectful relationship with an emotionally mature adult such as yourself.

Chapter 7:

Busting the Myths About Emotional Intelligence

As is the case with a lot of things, there exist several misconceptions regarding emotional intelligence. Throughout the course of this book, you've probably been able to identify the misconceptions you have had about emotional intelligence yourself, and the accompanying truth of the matter. This chapter is dedicated to busting the many myths that a whole lot of people have when it comes to EQ. Some of the myths are laughable, while others are downright ridiculous. Seeing that EQ deals with emotion, it is probably not too unexpected that there would be numerous feelings expressed on the same. Dive in to find out what is true about emotional intelligence and what isn't.

Myth: Emotional intelligence is a woman's area

Truth: Emotional intelligence is a skill that applies to both men and women.

For the longest time, the stereotype of women being more emotional than men has been perpetuated by various channels. It, therefore, follows that when most people hear of emotional intelligence, they only think of women. This could not be further from the truth. First of all, the claim that women are the more emotional of the human species is not a claim that is supported by biology. When scientists set out to study this phenomenon, they found out that the populations observed were more likely to behave according to the expectations placed on them by their cultures rather than as dictated by nature. In other words, women might behave more emotionally since that is what society or culture dictates from them, while men might repress their emotions for the same reason.

Seeing that we are capable of emotion, regardless of gender, it follows that there is a need to understand and manage those emotions. Even if there was a parallel universe where males were virtually incapable of having emotions, they would still be required to deal with women who, clearly, have emotions. As such, emotional intelligence is a scale that these parallel universe males would require when interacting with the parallel universe women.

Myth: Emotional intelligence is the sole determinant of success in life.

Truth: There are many factors that determine whether you will be successful in life, and EQ happens to be one of them.

Emotional intelligence opens a lot of doors for you in life. When you are able to read and relate well with people, you do not have as many obstacles when compared to someone who has low EQ. However, EQ is not the all-inclusive package for success. Success requires a combination of smarts, hard work, opportunity or chance, and sometimes even sheer luck. Being low in the EQ does not automatically qualify you for failure. In fact, there are some professions where people become highly successful just by relying on their IQ.

An engineer, for instance, might be required to have a very high IQ so that they can easily grasp concepts. The same engineer might be very low on the EQ front and still go on to become highly successful because their work calls for smarts over emotional intelligence. Sure, the engineer might struggle with personal relationships and will probably never hold a management position, but they will still be successful in their own right.

Myth: Emotional intelligence is about being nice.

Truth: Emotional intelligence is more than just being nice.

Over the years, nice has grown to be synonymous with being a pushover or a doormat. Whenever people hear that someone is nice, they start to imagine all manner of ways they can walk all over that person. Here's the thing: If you think of nice as the capacity to tolerate people's personalities and their idiosyncrasies, then yes, emotional intelligence is about being nice. However, if your definition of nice is the person that says yes to every request and does not have a voice of their own, then you are way off from what emotional intelligence actually is. Emotional intelligence does not make you a yes-man. In fact, emotional intelligence equips you with all the skills that you need to be able to say no as many times as you need and to do so unapologetically.

Myth: You're either born with emotional intelligence or not.

Truth: You can learn to become more emotionally intelligent.

Emotional intelligence is not the same as height whereby you are either born tall or short and are thereafter doomed to never reaching the higher shelves or always being the brunt of height jokes. Sure, some people have a higher ability to grasp emotional intelligence. This might depend on how they are born, how they are raised, the experiences they have been through, and numerous other factors that they interact with as they become adults. However, most people are capable of being emotionally intelligent. Even psychopaths who are incapable of feeling emotions like the rest of us know how to mimic emotional intelligence. If you are a fully functional human being with a wide range of emotions, then you are fully capable of being emotionally intelligent.

Myth: Everyone that knows how to charm people is emotionally intelligent.

Truth: Sometimes, there is more than emotional intelligence behind the charm.

Some of the most charming people you know are also the most dangerous human beings that you'll ever cross paths with. Just because a person knows when and how to smile in your face does not mean that they are high in EQ. They might just be manipulative. Psychopaths, for instance, know how to blend in and play Mr. Sociable Guy role to perfection. While an emotionally intelligent person will make you feel relaxed and comfortable without invading your personal space, a psychopath that is trying to win your trust may be more forceful, persistent, and full-on in a manner that might be uncomfortable. A trick you can use to determine whether you are dealing with high EQ or psychopathy is by trusting your gut feeling, watching whether someone's actions match their words, and noticing how you feel after every interaction. If you are leaving conversations feeling drained and unsure, you might be dealing with an energy vampire in the form of a psychopath rather than an emotionally intelligent person.

Myth: Introverts are not usually emotionally intelligent.

Truth: Introverts can be as emotionally intelligent as anyone else.

Introverts are known (or at least stereotyped) to be these shy and socially awkward people who have little to zero chance of ever being good at normal social interactions. While there may be some truth to it, this is not exactly the textbook definition of an introvert. An introvert is simply someone who prefers to look into themselves rather than turning to their external world for stimulation. An introvert is content in their own company and will often prefer to be silent rather than to talk. An introvert's worst nightmare is the extrovert, especially the kind of extrovert who does not have any emotional intelligence. Now, just because a person prefers to be silent does not mean that they are low in emotional intelligence. In fact, the fact that introverts are inward-looking means that they probably already have the self-awareness bit of EQ figured out. However, because introverts tend to be so absorbed in their worlds (in the most unselfish way possible), it means that they have to work a little harder at drawing themselves out into their external environment.

Seeing that introversion is a personality type, and personalities are not known scientifically to be dynamic, an introvert will often face the uphill task of opening up their world to other people. For instance, you cannot be empathetic to the suffering of others unless you are aware of this suffering. To become aware of this suffering, you must at least speak with this person so that they can tell you that yes, indeed they are having a bad day. This can be almost too much to ask from an introvert.

The good news is that emotional intelligence can be learned since it is a skill like any other. An introvert is able to pick up the cues that they need to incorporate to be emotionally intelligent, just like all other personality types. In fact, there are introverts out there who are highly emotionally intelligent. They know how to carry themselves when they are in a group of people. They understand that certain circumstances call for them to leave the security of their shells. Once they are back home, they quietly retreat to the safety of their shell until further circumstances require them to come out.

Myth: Emotional intelligence is only important for people in leadership roles or in particular professions.

Truth: Emotional intelligence makes your life easier regardless of who you are.

When you are in a leadership position, your lack of emotional intelligence will be more apparent and detrimental compared to a lack of emotional intelligence in the people that you lead or any other person. It has been said that with great power comes great responsibility, and this could not be truer when it comes to emotional intelligence. When you serve as a leader or boss, your every move is in the spotlight. People will pay attention to how you speak to your juniors, how you show care and consideration for others, how you manage stressful situations, and even how you manage yourself. Your teams will also look to you to model the kind of behavior that they should emulate and to be their mentor in matters of business and relationships. Imagine being in such a position while lacking emotional intelligence. More likely than not, you are going to be highly overwhelmed.

That being said, everyone needs emotional intelligence in their lives. You do not need to be anybody's boss to appreciate the benefits that come with being self-aware and self-regulating. And what about motivation? Everyone could use some bit of intrinsic drive and passion in their lives. Motivation is what gives you the fuel to get you everything that you need in your life. If not for anything else, aim to be emotionally intelligent so that you can have better personal relationships in your life. We could all use some of those.

Chapter 8:

Are You Emotionally Intelligent?

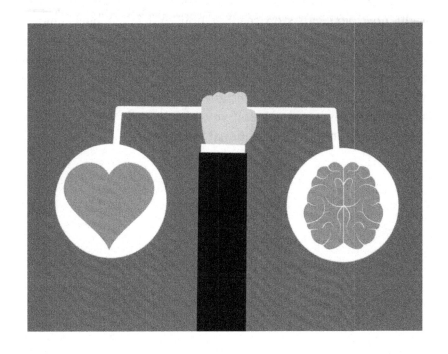

Congratulations on making it to the last chapter of this book. In this chapter, you'll have the chance to evaluate your emotional intelligence and see how well you measure up. Most likely, you were able to identify areas for self-improvement along the way as you read this book. The quiz below is intended to help you gain even more clarity on what your strong areas are and where your weaknesses lie as far as emotional intelligence is concerned. If the results show that you are emotionally intelligent, then you can keep doing what you have been doing. If, at the end of the test, you realize that you have not been behaving in a manner that is emotionally intelligent, then this is not something that should make you feel bad. Rather, this should serve as motivation for you to do better and be better.

Feel free to start this test whenever you are ready. If it is not right now, you can stop reading now and come back later, or jump to the conclusion, quite literally. If you are ready to take the quiz now, then proceed. The rules of the test are simple. Answer *true* or *false* to the statements below and then tally your score at the end. Remember to be truthful with your answers. You must remain objective and honest if you wish to truly get a reasonably accurate picture of your emotional intelligence.

Emotional Intelligence Quiz

1.   You are able to identify what you are feeling most of the time and use extensive vocabulary to label it. You do not just say you are fine or not fine. Rather, you can clearly tell when you are feeling frustrated, disappointed, angry, overwhelmed, sad, and so on. TRUE/FALSE

2.   You have never thought of yourself as self-absorbed, selfish, or self-serving to the point where you do not care about what is going on around you. You are naturally curious to find out more about the people around you. Even if you are on the introverted side, you are happy to just observe to learn more about the people you meet in your everyday life. TRUE/FALSE

3.   You adapt easily to change. You are flexible in your thinking, and you believe that change is as good as rest. You consider a change to be one of the more exciting things about life. TRUE/FALSE

4.   You are well aware of what your strengths are and can also clearly articulate your weakness. You know the people you get along with and the people who tend to grate on your nerves. TRUE/FALSE

5.   You are not easily fooled by people. You can easily judge a person's character even when they are trying to pass themselves off as something else. When it comes to people, very few things catch you by surprise. TRUE/FALSE

6.   You consider yourself to have a pretty thick skin. You do not walk around looking for things to be offended about. You are able to appreciate self-deprecating humor

and do not mind being the butt of a joke unless it crosses respectable boundaries. TRUE/FALSE

7. You learn from your mistakes without wallowing in them. You know that it is human to make mistakes from time to time. You see failure as an opportunity to learn and not as an indication of your self-worth. TRUE/FALSE

8. You forgive those who have wronged you because you understand that it is the right thing to do for yourself. Grudges have no place in your life, and you move on easily from other people's transgressions against you. TRUE/FALSE

9. Whenever you have to interact with a toxic person, you know how to handle them in a way that doesn't drain you emotionally. You try as much as possible to see things from the toxic person's perspective, however difficult this might be. You know how to protect your energy while handling toxic persons. TRUE/FALSE

10. You do not pursue perfection because you understand that it is just a concept that exists in people's minds and not in reality. You do not demand perfection from yourself or your loved ones or even the people you work with. You simply want to be able to say that you did your best under the circumstances that you were in. TRUE/FALSE

11. You know when you need to take a break from the stresses of everyday life, and you do so unapologetically. You have never felt obliged to be available to everyone and everything 24/7. You can switch off and unwind easily because you know it is important for your overall health as a physical, mental, and emotional being. TRUE/FALSE

12. You are cautious about what you allow inside your body. You know that what you eat has a significant role in how you feel and know better than to allow toxic stuff into your system. You watch what you eat without being obsessive about it. TRUE/FALSE.

13. You consider sleep to be a priority. You do not stay up all night doing things that can be postponed to tomorrow. You know that sleep is an important part of your life because it allows your brain to rest and recharge. You tend to sleep at the same time every night. TRUE/FALSE.

14. You speak kindly to yourself. Negative self-talk has no place in your life. You do not allow yourself to be harsh or judgmental toward yourself. You forgive yourself for your mistakes and look for ways to improve yourself instead of beating yourself up for every flaw that you might have. TRUE/FALSE

15. You are confident in who you are and do not look to others for validation. You are proud of your accomplishments and know-how to celebrate your wins, big and small. You do not lose your sleep over other people's opinions because you know the opinion that truly matters is what you think about yourself. You do not allow anyone to come into your life to steal away your joy. TRUE/FALSE

How many questions did you answer TRUE to? The table below shows how you are faring on the emotional intelligence scale based on your answers.

Questions that you have answered TRUE to	EQ Rating	What this means
15	Very High EQ	You are in tune with your emotions, are grounded in your identity as an individual, and highly motivated to be true to yourself. You respect other people and their emotions without allowing them to take over your life. You are probably fun to be around because you are emotionally mature and can handle a joke or two. Your friends and colleagues actually do like you more than you think. Not that this matters to you anyway. Popular or not, you're content in who you are and would not change, only improve.
10-14	High EQ	You know who you are and you know how to read others. You are empathetic toward other people, but you also do not allow them to steal your energy. You appreciate the importance of being emotionally intelligent and will

		always bite your tongue before you can lash out at anyone. You like yourself and can clearly articulate what your goals, dreams, and achievements are. You have opinions about things, but you also accommodate differing opinions without getting worked up.
5-9	Average EQ	You get along with most people, and you like yourself on most days. However, you still struggle with a lot of things regarding yourself and your emotions and other people. You have good days when you seem to do and say the right things and bad days when your foot is constantly in your mouth. Sometimes you are too hard on yourself, and you have moments when you wish you could go back in time and fix the mistakes you have made. You take too long to forgive yourself and others, and you have some bad blood that you are still holding onto. You wish you could be a better person; you just do not know-how. (Hopefully, this book has

		answered how.)
0-4	Low EQ	If your life was made into a television show, it would be a bad sitcom that would get canceled after one season. You do not have a clear view of who you are. You seem to offend everyone everywhere you go. You feel lousy about yourself and your life constantly. You struggle to get up for work every morning. Your colleagues do not seem to like you very much, and your boss is probably considering firing you. You struggle with dating, and if you are in a relationship or married, then you cannot seem to stop your partner from arguing with you. You yell when you get angry, and you've even thrown a few items in the heat of the moment. The emotions in your life show up in their extreme forms. You are never just happy or relaxed. You are more likely to be extremely angry/agitated/frustrated than just moderately feeling those emotions. There are opportunities and hope for you

		to become more emotionally intelligent, but it calls for you to work really hard at resolving all the issues that you currently have.

Table 3: Emotional Intelligence Rating

Conclusion

How do you think you did on the test in Chapter 8? Do you feel like it is an accurate representation of who you are? How did it feel reading through what your EQ score means? Did you feel attacked and unworthy, or were you vindicated as the emotionally intelligent person that you have always believed yourself to be? The simple test in Chapter 8 was not meant to make you look bad or feel as if you are unworthy of any kindness. You may be the most well-meaning person and still score poorly in emotional intelligence because of your experiences and even your personality. Perhaps you are a shy person that is often unable to make conversation easily. Does that mean you are the worst person in the world? Does it mean that being socially awkward means you'll never be able to land your dream job because the hiring managers want people high in EQ?

Not necessarily.

A reassuring fact about emotional intelligence is that you can be terrible at it in January and get better by March. It is as simple as picking up the components of EQ discussed in this book and incorporating them into your life. How hard can it be to be a good listener? Not too hard. You just have to sit there and nod attentively while keeping your eyes trained on the speaker. And empathy? Well, a whole lot of empathy is knowing when not to say a stupid thing. Next time your friend gets heartbroken, do not rush to remind them that there is plenty of fish in the sea. Allow them to mourn the fish that they have just lost while you stand behind them like the good friend that you are, patting them on their back and reminding them that they are the prettiest, smartest dolphin in the sea and anybody would be lucky to have them.

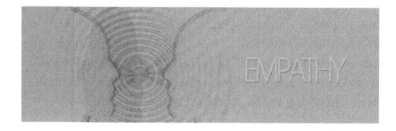

Author Note

Thank you for reading one of my books! This is the first book I've written since 2019. It took me years to decide to write it, mostly because I couldn't get out of my way. I worked in the IT department for 20 years. However, in 2017 I set a goal to start to write a book I'd begun writing a long time ago.

The desire to write this book was because I wanted to be able to help people have inner growth as I have done in the last ten years.

The problems had in the family, at work, and in everyday life, led me to make a path of growth in Emotional Intelligence. Seeing the significant improvements that I had, I felt the desire to write a book to give other people a starting point for a better quality of life.

I hope this book has given you some stimulus to start personal growth.

I would like you to be able to dedicate 5 minutes of your precious time to leave a review. The reviews are very important for me because I can understand what you think of my book. Receive valuable advice that will surely help me improve it.

Simply scan the QR code to be able to write your review directly.

Brandon Goleman

Table of Contents

References

Bernstein, A. (2012). Emotional Vampires: Dealing With People Who Drain You Dry (2nd ed.). New York: McGraw-Hill.

Gallagher, D., & Costal, J. (2012). *The Self-Aware Leader*. Alexandria, Va.: ASTD Press.

Gender and emotional expression. (2019). Retrieved from https://en.wikipedia.org/wiki/Gender_and_emotional_expression

Goleman, D. (2012). *Emotional Intelligence: Why It Can Matter More Than IQ*. (10th Anniv. ed.). Random House Publishing Group.

Howe, D. (2013). *Empathy: What It Is and Why It Matters*. Houndmills, Basingstoke, Hampshire: Palgrave Macmillan.

Plutchik, Robert (2002), *Emotions and Life: Perspectives from Psychology, Biology, and Evolution*. Washington, DC: American Psychological Association.

Emotional Intelligence

Brandon Goleman

Introduction

We couldn't possibly begin to understand how the first humans perceived each other. They might not have always gotten along, but soon realized the importance of working together to survive. As their brains developed and time went on, they may have found redeeming qualities among one another, especially in reference to mating, as well as understanding the many differences they possessed despite their appearance.

All we have are scientific theories and speculation. It is generally believed (and yet very poorly discussed) that Homo Sapiens ruled over other species of humans because they were fierce and, well, a lot less ethical. These beings saw nothing wrong with eliminating any other species that threatened them for the sake of land ownership and, later on, cultivation (Harari, 2019).

It seems we have always been complex beings, torn between ourselves and our communities, between the different groups we belonged to, and, ultimately, between our physical bodies and moral compass.

There is a very good reason ancient Greeks encouraged the discovery of our inner selves. The key to a happy life lies beyond the material or social groups, but in how you know and trust yourself. The moment we accept that we are complex creatures that won't ever fit into predefined molds (nor should we want to) is the moment we are set free and can truly embrace our authentic abilities.

The book at hand will discuss just that: being authentic in a world that seems to duplicate personalities like a Xerox machine that works day and night. We know how a "perfect" home should look, and just how many pounds we need to weigh to be considered beautiful in society's eyes. We know how to make the perfect pasta and how to "read" which high school clique to belong to, even though it's been three decades, and doesn't hold power anymore.

We know too little about ourselves. And what's even worse, we know almost nothing about what it means to love the person underneath the facade. When you pertain to typology that is often looked at from extreme perspectives, this makes it even more difficult. Other people will either vilify or glorify you without permission, and little by little, you might start to believe their narrative.

Take empaths, for example. You know how difficult it is to live among people with so many different emotions if you are an empath. You also know, deep inside, that this is a gift, a super-power. Yet, in a society that glorifies the ultra-strong, being sensitive is frequently seen as a weakness or a problem that needs to be fixed, rather than a gift to be embraced.

Empaths come in all the colors of the rainbow. You might pertain to a more extreme category, and you might feel suffocated every time you go out to face a wall of emotions that do not belong to you. You might be a more moderate empath who can function well even in the larger groups.

Wherever you are on this scale, you have likely been told, at least once, that you are *too sensitive*. It might have been a parent, a mentor, your first friend in the world, or your worst enemy. It might have been your abuser, your lover, a coworker, or your boss. Whoever it was, they most likely said it like this is something you need to alter in your personality and way of being.

Well, this book is here to show you the opposite. You do not have to fix your sensitivity. You have to learn how to manage it and how to embrace it as a gift. Empaths can see the world in more colors and flavors that others will never get to experience. They can help so many people; it's almost incredible they are not more celebrated in society. And they can create the kind of art that touches the soul for centuries.

Empaths are truly amazing beings. Unfortunately, they are often those who are the most misunderstood (even by themselves). They are easily hurt and might flip their personality as a result.

To understand an empath, you must first understand the very concept of complexity. Instead of feeling the need to put them into a box with a label, we should take the time to understand this psychological typology as the one that might be our salvation as a species. We need to learn the kindness of an empath and their ability to transcend beyond social norms, religions, and physical borders. We need to embrace our empaths and protect them.

If you are an empath seeking to understand yourself, you should also take the time to understand complexity (and, more specifically, the complex range of emotions you might experience, as well as how easy it is for these emotions to shift towards the negative).

This book will place empaths at its core. As such, we will start off with a chapter designed to offer more information about empaths: what they are, how they are most often defined, the different degrees of the empathy scale, as well as the downsides of being an empath and why it is important to control these pitfalls.

The second chapter will cover acceptance. Learning how to embrace your empathy is extremely important for the development of harmony and happiness as a person - which can be a life-saver for some. As such, we have dedicated a pretty extensive topic on the topic of how you can embrace your typology and make the most out of it.

The third chapter of this book is where things get even more interesting. As mentioned before, people are far too complex to fit into predefined molds. We will debate the intricate relationship between narcissistic personality disorder, empaths, and emotional intelligence as the liaison between the two. As you will see, there is a lot more to empaths and their connection to narcissists than most people believe.

Lastly, we will demystify some of the most common inaccurate things people believe but aren't necessarily true about empaths. As you will read in this last chapter, empaths and narcissists should not always be seen as complete opposites of each other, as their personalities might sometimes intermingle.

This book's primary goal is to help you understand yourself as an empath (if you are one) or someone close to you who is an empath. I believe the key to a better world is by paying attention to how we treat ourselves and each other - and as such, I believe empaths should be empowered with the things they need to make the most out of their talent and help the rest of us connect.

Empaths are one of the most fascinating psychological typologies there is. Distant and frequently socially awkward, empaths are a gift we must all treasure precisely because they possess qualities nobody else has - such as the ability to read between the lines and beyond the appearance of a human being as well as establishing a true kinship.

I hope I can be of real help to you and your loved ones. The information collected in these pages is meant to support further research and self-education, as well as a healthy jump-start into a life-long journey of self-love and gratitude.

Hopefully, by the end, you will know more about yourself, what makes you tick, and how to protect yourself from negative influences and potentially hurtful interactions.

I wish you all the best in this journey of self-discovery, and I genuinely hope it will help you become the best version of yourself. Because, as an empath, you deserve nothing less!

Brandon Goleman 2019

Last update May 2020

Made in the USA
Monee, IL
08 April 2021

65086599R00069